About the Authors

Paul N. Weinberg

Paul Weinberg received a B.S. degree from the University of Michigan and an M.S. degree from Stanford University, both in computer science. He has held software development and marketing positions at Bell Laboratories, Hewlett-Packard, and Plexus Computers. Mr. Weinberg is currently vice president and cofounder of Network Innovations, a supplier of PC/UNIX networking software. He is the author of several technical articles on UNIX software and performance measurement, which have appeared in *PC Magazine*, *Mini-Micro Systems*, and *Unique*. While at Stanford, he collaborated on *The Simple Solution to Rubik's Cube*, the best-selling book of 1981, with over seven million copies in print.

James R. Groff

Jim Groff received a B.S. degree in mathematics from the Massachusetts Institute of Technology and an M.B.A. degree from Harvard University. He has published a number of technical articles on the UNIX system and UNIX networking in *Electronics, Systems and Software*, and *Mini-Micro Systems*. Mr. Groff is president and cofounder of Network Innovations, and was previously director of marketing at Plexus Computers. He has also held a number of marketing positions at Hewlett-Packard, where he was responsible for the HP 100 series of personal computers.

Understanding XENIX
A Conceptual Guide

Paul N. Weinberg
James R. Groff

Que Corporation
Indianapolis

Library of Congress Catalog No.: LC 84-62751
ISBN 0-88022-143-7

Editor
Virginia D. Noble, M.L.S.

Editorial Director
David F. Noble, Ph.D.

Composed in Megaron by
Que Corporation

Printed and bound by
George Banta Co., Inc.

Cover designed by
Listenberger Design Associates

Table of Contents

8 TURNKEY PROCESSING WITH XENIX

Foreword

Understanding XENIX describes the features and utilities available with most versions of the XENIX system. The examples used throughout this book are applicable to XENIX Version 3, which is available on the IBM PC AT.

For readability, the names of programs, utilities, and files are set in boldface type. When a user interaction with the system is displayed, computer prompts and responses are set in plain type, and user input is set in boldface type. When the contents of a file are reproduced in the text, they also appear in boldface type. Comments are included beside the appropriate line, on the right-hand side, following a pound sign (#).

Preface

With the introduction of the IBM PC AT in August of 1984, the XENIX operating system has leaped to prominence. *Understanding XENIX* is designed to help you understand the role of XENIX in the world of personal computers and the important trend toward multiuser microcomputer systems.

The goal of this book is to provide a top-down, conceptual view of the XENIX system and its place in the world of computer software. This text is unlike the XENIX tutorials or XENIX introductions you may have considered buying or may already own. Our goal is not to provide a terminal aid for a new XENIX user, with step-by-step instructions on what to type next. Nor is our goal to make you a proficient C programmer using XENIX. Instead, this text presents an overall perspective of the XENIX system and the concepts that make it unique. In other words, this book seeks to answer these questions: What is XENIX, and why is it suddenly attracting so much attention?

Understanding XENIX is an appropriate text for anyone seeking technical or market insights into the XENIX system. We assume that readers have some level of familiarity with computers and computer ideas. If you've used a personal computer, read a lot about computers, or come into contact with them at work, you should have no trouble understanding the concepts in this book. We specifically do not assume that you have had any prior experience with the XENIX system.

In some of the chapters, the subject matter is explored at two different levels. These chapters are structured so that each one begins with a complete, high-level exposition of the topic. More advanced information is covered in later sections, each of which is marked with an asterisk to signify an *advanced topic.* You do not need to read these sections to obtain an understanding of what XENIX is and what it does. These sections present material that is important to computer professionals who need to know about the internal structure of the XENIX system.

Understanding XENIX is organized topically. Chapter 1 introduces the XENIX system and presents its major features and their benefits. Chapter 2 provides an overview of XENIX's role as a potential standard operating system for multiuser microcomputers. This chapter includes the history and development of the XENIX system. Chapter 3 compares XENIX to other versions of UNIX and to MS-DOS.

The structure of the XENIX system is examined in Chapter 4. It identifies the major components of XENIX and explains their functions, benefits, and interrelationships.

One of the most powerful features of XENIX is the XENIX file system, discussed in Chapter 5. This chapter describes the file system facilities for organizing and managing stored information, and for controlling system input and output. Chapter 6 describes the shell, which is the XENIX system's command interpreter. For many users the shell *is* XENIX because it is the primary interface for the XENIX system.

Chapters 7 and 8 describe the features that make the XENIX operating system an excellent choice for multiuser computer systems. Chapter 7 examines multiuser operation from the user's perspective. And Chapter 8 covers the underlying structures that make XENIX an excellent foundation for building turnkey applications, where XENIX itself is invisible to the application user.

The next several chapters describe the four major areas in which XENIX offers a wealth of utility programs. Chapter 9 describes the utilities for file processing and data processing. XENIX tools that support text processing and office automation are covered in Chapter 10. XENIX has also earned an excellent reputation as a software development environment, and relevant tools for this application are described in Chapter 11. Chapter 12 outlines the XENIX utilities that support computer-to-computer communications.

Finally, Chapter 13 deals with trends in the market for XENIX-based systems and software, as well as the future of XENIX itself. The market for XENIX-based systems and software is exploding. The market entry of IBM makes it even more essential for you to understand the forces behind the XENIX phenomenon.

Acknowledgments

The authors wish to thank the following individuals who provided information and assistance in the writing of this book: Bruce Steinberg of The Santa Cruz Operation, Jerry Dunietz of Microsoft Corporation, Rosemary Morrissey and Thomas Ternus of International Business Machines Corporation, and Bob Marsh of Plexus Computers, Inc.

Trademark Acknowledgments

Altos is a registered trademark of Altos Computer Systems.

Apple is a trademark of Apple Computer, Inc.

AT&T is a registered trademark of American Telephone and Telegraph Corporation.

Coherent is a trademark of Mark Williams Company.

CP/M, CP/M-86, and Digital Research are registered trademarks of Digital Research, Inc.

Cromemco and Cromix are registered trademarks of Cromemco, Inc.

dBASE II is a registered trademark of Ashton-Tate. Ashton-Tate is a trademark of Ashton-Tate.

General Electric is a registered trademark of General Electric Company.

Hewlett-Packard is a registered trademark of Hewlett-Packard Company.

IBM is a registered trademark of International Business Machines Corporation.

Intel is a registered trademark of Intel Corporation.

MicroPro is a registered trademark of MicroPro International Corporation.

Motorola ia a registered trademark of Motorola, Inc.

Multiplan and Microsoft are registered trademarks of Microsoft Corporation. XENIX and MS are trademarks of Microsoft Corporation.

National Semiconductor is a registered trademark of National Semiconductor Corporation.

PDP-11, Digital, and VAX are trademarks of Digital Equipment Corporation.

Poppy is a trademark of Durango Systems, Inc.

Radio Shack and TRS-80 are registered trademarks of Radio Shack Corporation.

Tandy and TRS are registered trademarks of Tandy Corporation.

UCSD p-System is a trademark of the Board of Regents of the University of California.

uNETix is a registered trademark of LanTech Systems, Inc.

UniPlus+ and UniSoft are registered trademarks of UniSoft Systems.

UNIX is a trademark of Bell Laboratories, Inc.

VisiCorp is a registered trademark of VisiCorp.

Wicat is a registered trademark of Wicat Systems, Inc.

Z80 and Zilog are registered trademarks of Zilog, Inc.

Que Corporation has made every attempt to supply trademark information about company names, products, and services mentioned in this book. Trademarks indicated were derived from various sources. Que Corporation cannot attest to the accuracy of this information.

1

Introduction

The introduction of high-performance 32-bit microprocessors is one of the most important developments in the computer industry of the mid-1980s. This new generation of processors brings with it a quantum increase in processing power—the proverbial "mainframe on a desktop." These processors make possible not only advanced personal computers, but low-cost *multiuser* systems as well. The IBM PC AT, introduced in August of 1984, is the most prominent of these systems and signals the opening of a mass market for multiuser "supermicro" systems.

Over the last several years, the XENIX operating system has established itself as the most widely installed operating system on low-cost multiuser systems. IBM's endorsement of XENIX as the multiuser operating system of choice for the IBM PC AT has cemented this leadership position. The endorsement has also fueled speculation that XENIX will become the next industry-standard operating system, playing the same role for sophisticated multiuser micros that MS-DOS has assumed for personal computers such as the IBM PC.

The role of XENIX in the exploding market for supermicro systems is a controversial one. XENIX advocates speak of its "elegance, power, and simplicity" and seem confident of its claim to industry-standard status. Critics, on the other hand, charge that XENIX is too cryptic and unfriendly to gain widespread acceptance on micro-computers. Others foresee the obsolescence of XENIX as multiuser systems give way to networks of personal computers.

Exactly what is XENIX? How does it compare to MS-DOS as an op-erating system for personal computers? How does XENIX relate to UNIX and its various versions, such as UNIX System V, Berkeley UNIX, and PC/IX? What are some of XENIX's major features and benefits? How do XENIX-based multiuser systems compare to net-works of PCs for office applications? Finally, what is the role of XENIX in the microcomputer marketplace today, and what role is it likely to play in the future?

Understanding XENIX presents a conceptual overview of the XENIX system and its place in the computer industry. This book topically describes XENIX's main features and their benefits, with many easy-to-understand examples. *Understanding XENIX* also relates XENIX to the overall "UNIX phenomenon." In summary, this book gives you the information you need to assess personally the significance of XENIX and its impact on you and your business.

The XENIX Operating System

XENIX is the name of an operating system created by Microsoft Cor-poration for multiuser microcomputer systems. XENIX is a version of UNIX, which is a minicomputer operating system originally de-veloped at Bell Laboratories. To create XENIX, Microsoft enhanced and extended UNIX, adapting it for use on microcomputers and add-ing features that make it better suited for commercial applications.

An *operating system* is the computer software that manages and controls the operation of a computer system. The operating system controls the computer hardware, manages system resources, runs programs in response to user commands, and supervises the inter-action between the system and its users. The operating system also forms a foundation on which *applications software*—such as word-processing, spreadsheet, and accounting programs—is developed and executed.

The operating system of a computer is largely responsible for determining its personality and usefulness. Depending on the design of the operating system, it may be particularly well suited for certain applications and unsuited for others. The XENIX system is a general-purpose, multiuser operating system that is applicable to many different user environments.

The UNIX system from which XENIX was derived has long enjoyed a reputation as an excellent software development and document-processing environment. XENIX-based systems are also widely used for these applications. But the enhancements added to XENIX by Microsoft make the operating system well suited to commercial applications as well. Most XENIX-based systems today are installed in small businesses and used for accounting, inventory control, order entry, word processing, billing, and payroll.

XENIX is poorly suited to real-time applications, such as laboratory instrument control or factory automation. XENIX is also not generally used for engineering and scientific applications. Nor does XENIX play a significant role in the minicomputer or mainframe computer markets, though other versions of UNIX are quite successful on these systems.

XENIX and the UNIX Explosion

The growing importance of XENIX is part of a larger explosion in the market for UNIX-based computer systems over the last several years. Until recently, the UNIX system was available on only a handful of different computers. Most UNIX installations existed within the Bell System where UNIX originated. Widely regarded as a tool for academic institutions and research labs, UNIX was far removed from the "real world" of commercial applications.

Today, over one hundred different computer vendors offer products based on UNIX, XENIX, or UNIX "look-alikes." Industry forecasters predict that by 1986 the market for UNIX-based systems, software, and services will top several billion dollars annually. UNIX-based operating systems are available on a broader range of computer systems than that of any other operating system.

At the low end of the spectrum, versions of UNIX are now available for personal computers and "laptop" computers priced under

$3,000. Single-user versions of UNIX, such as PC/IX for the IBM PC XT and XENIX for the Apple Lisa, have turned these personal computers into powerful workstations for programmers and, to a lesser extent, into small business systems. But UNIX continues to play a secondary role in this market segment, which is dominated by the IBM PC and its MS-DOS operating system.

On larger multiuser microcomputers, XENIX and other versions of UNIX have become the industry-standard operating system. These supermicrocomputers offer performance which exceeds that of many minicomputers, at prices starting under $10,000. XENIX has had a major impact on these systems, accounting for the largest installed base of any UNIX version. XENIX is offered on the Radio Shack TRS-80 Model 16; the Altos 586 system; and, of course, the IBM PC AT. The sophisticated applications that are being developed for these systems make this segment the "hottest" of the UNIX market.

UNIX has had a tremendous impact on the minicomputer market as well. The "big three" minicomputer manufacturers—Digital Equipment Corporation, Data General, and Hewlett-Packard—have all announced UNIX systems for their popular minicomputer and superminicomputer product lines. On larger systems, UNIX is available for mainframes from IBM and Amdahl. UNIX will even be the standard operating system for the Cray-II, the most powerful supercomputer commercially available.

The UNIX explosion also extends to UNIX-based software. Several hundred different software packages are now available for use with UNIX, from language compilers to spreadsheet packages, and from word processors to a host of business applications. Some of these software products are upgraded versions of the simple packages developed for early personal computers. But the vast majority are more sophisticated, having been originally designed to run on minicomputers. These products are now available on a much broader range of computer equipment because of the proliferation of UNIX.

Major XENIX Features and Benefits

XENIX is a comprehensive operating system with an amazing number of features and capabilities. Its major features include the following:

- Portability/compatibility with UNIX
- Portable applications software
- Multiuser operation
- Background processing
- Hierarchical file system
- The XENIX shell
- The visual shell
- Pipes
- Utilities
- Text-processing tools
- Software development tools
- Maturity
- Commercial extensions to UNIX

This set of features is cited by XENIX advocates as the reason why XENIX is emerging as the standard operating system for powerful multiuser microcomputer systems.

Portability and Compatibility with UNIX

XENIX is easily adapted to run on different computer systems. Moving XENIX to a new system typically requires only a few man-months of effort. XENIX is also compatible with the various versions of UNIX. As a result, UNIX and XENIX have rapidly become available on a wide range of computer hardware. Customers can purchase UNIX/ XENIX systems from over a hundred different hardware vendors, without being "locked in" to a single supplier. This *vendor independence* is a major benefit of the UNIX/XENIX proliferation.

Portable Applications Software

Besides the XENIX system itself, the applications software written for XENIX is also portable. The same UNIX/XENIX-based applications can run on micros, minis, and mainframes. Software suppliers can offer their software solutions on a broad spectrum of systems with different capacities and performances. Customers can choose the hardware and software combination that best meets their application needs.

Multiuser Operation

XENIX is a multiuser system, designed to support a group of simultaneous users. The system allows efficient sharing of the processing power and the information storage of a computer system, while offering the security and protection features needed to insulate each user from the activities of other users. XENIX-based systems, with their ability to support many users working with common data and their low cost per user, are ideally suited for use in smaller businesses and departments of larger companies.

Background Processing

XENIX supports *background* processing, which allows a user to initiate a task and then proceed to other activities while the system continues to work on the original task. For example, the system can be sorting a file and printing a report on a user's behalf at the same time that the user is editing a document. Background processing helps users to be more effective in using the system and accomplishing more work in a given period of time.

Hierarchical File System

XENIX features a *hierarchical file system* for organizing stored information. The hierarchical structure offers maximum flexibility for grouping information in a way that reflects its natural structure. A single user's data, for example, may be grouped by activity. And data from many different users can be grouped according to corporate organization. As a result, stored data is easier to locate and manage.

The XENIX Shell

User interaction with XENIX is controlled by the *shell*, a powerful command interpreter. The shell supports a number of convenient features, such as the ability to redirect application input and output, and the ability to manipulate groups of files with a single command. The shell also supports execution of predefined command sequences in conjunction with built-in programming language features. These capabilities allow even complex tasks to be performed by unsophisticated users.

The Visual Shell

XENIX also includes an alternative user interface called the *visual shell*. The visual shell is menu-driven and simplifies XENIX operation for novice users. Its full-screen display resembles that of Microsoft's PC applications packages, such as Multiplan. The visual shell's menus provide access to the most frequently used XENIX commands for file management, text processing, and electronic mail.

Pipes

One of the most famous UNIX features included in XENIX is the *pipe*. Pipes are used to combine several simple programs to perform more complex functions. In many cases, new tasks require only that existing programs and utilities be combined using pipes, thus eliminating the need for new software development.

XENIX Utilities

XENIX includes over two hundred utility programs for functions like sorting data, processing text, and searching for information. These utilities form a powerful collection of tools that can be used to accomplish many tasks without writing new programs.

Text-Processing Tools

XENIX offers a rich assortment of tools for all aspects of text processing. Text-editing utilities support the creation, editing, and management of documents. Text-formatting utilities generate output for a wide range of printing devices, from draft-quality printers to phototypesetters.

Software Development Tools

UNIX is widely recognized as an excellent system for software development. XENIX includes UNIX's extensive array of software tools that support all phases of the development process, from program editing through debugging. In addition, XENIX includes specialized cross-development tools for creating MS-DOS-based applications.

As a result, XENIX is widely used to develop systems and applications software for computers, from micros to mainframes.

Maturity

XENIX is derived from UNIX, a solid, time-tested operating system that has been in use for over fourteen years. The software is mature and relatively free of bugs, offering a high level of reliability for an operating system of its capability.

Commercial Extensions to UNIX

UNIX is often criticized for its lack of certain key features that are required for use in commercial data processing environments. In XENIX, Microsoft has addressed these deficiencies by adding such capabilities as record locking, synchronous writes, shared memory, and simplified system administration. XENIX has also been specifically tailored and performance-tuned for use on microprocessor-based systems.

2

A XENIX Perspective

Much of the attention that XENIX has attracted derives from its potential status as a new industry-standard microcomputer operating system. What does it mean to be a standard operating system? What advantages are offered by a standard? How can XENIX be a standard when it is but one of many different versions of UNIX? And how did XENIX achieve its status of widespread acceptance and use? This chapter examines the evolution of standard operating systems and traces the history of both UNIX and XENIX.

Standards in the Computer Industry

The notion of a standard operating system is a relatively new one in the computer industry. In the 1970s the fastest growing part of the industry was composed of minicomputer manufacturers, each offering nonstandard, proprietary products. While these manufacturers were developing their hardware and software products, each claimed the "best" processor, computer languages, and operating system. In choosing a vendor, a customer "locked himself in" to one

9

manufacturer's gear because the costs of changing to another, incompatible system were prohibitive.

In contrast, the microcomputer era of the 1980s can be accurately called the "era of standards." True, hundreds of microcomputer systems are available. But each is powered by one of a mere handful of standard microprocessors. Microcomputer peripherals are standardized, too. Disks, for example, come in 8-inch and 5 1/4-inch standard sizes, with standard capacities and standard ways of connecting them to systems. Standard microcomputer operating systems have emerged as well.

Standard operating systems offer the following unique advantages to all participants in the microcomputer market:

- Customers benefit because they are no longer captive to a single manufacturer.
- Applications developers benefit because they can offer their software on a wide range of different systems.
- Computer manufacturers benefit from more rapid acceptance of their products and through reduced software development costs.

In fact, the development of standards may be the single largest contributor to the explosive growth of the microcomputer market.

CP/M—The First Standard Operating System

Any discussion of standard operating systems must begin with CP/M, the first standard operating system for microcomputers. CP/M (Control Program for Microcomputers) was developed in the 1970s for an early 8-bit microprocessor, the Intel 8080. Although the 8080 was popular from the start, software development for microcomputers was a tedious process in those days. Without the help of systems software, applications programs had to perform for themselves many low-level functions, such as input/output control (for instance, directly reading characters typed on the keyboard or handling the movement of a disk drive's recording head). Yet main memory was too precious to support the big operating systems that were typical of minicomputers.

Recognizing that the lack of systems software was a barrier to rapid development of the market, early microcomputer manufacturers seized on CP/M when it was introduced by Digital Research. CP/M offered a good compromise operating system for the microcomputers of the day because of the following distinctions:

- It was small, requiring only about 8K of main memory.
- It handled low-level input/output tasks, freeing programmers to concentrate on their applications.
- It was portable, with hardware-specific functions concentrated in one small part of the software.
- It was simple and easy to learn.

Adoption of CP/M by a few early microcomputer manufacturers set in motion the "standardization cycle" depicted in figure 2.1. Availability of CP/M-based systems attracted software vendors to write CP/M-based applications. Availability of these applications meant that more customers could buy solutions to their word-processing and accounting problems, and other problems as well. Increased sales of systems attracted into the market more manufacturers who selected CP/M as their operating system. In a short time, therefore, CP/M became the standard operating system for 8-bit microprocessors, with hundreds of computer systems and thousands of applications packages based on it.

MS-DOS—The Standard for 16-Bit PCs

With CP/M firmly established as the dominant 8-bit operating system, the summer of 1981 produced a milestone event in the microcomputer market. IBM introduced the IBM PC, which had a 16-bit microprocessor, the Intel 8088. With this processor, the IBM PC leapfrogged the established market.

It is easy to forget how different the personal computer market of 1981 was from the market of today. Apple and Tandy, with their own proprietary operating systems, were the largest personal computer manufacturers. The other smaller manufacturers were clustered around CP/M. Of the major computer companies, only XEROX had introduced a personal computer product, and it too was based on CP/M. Hewlett-Packard had introduced its CP/M-based system the day before the IBM announcement.

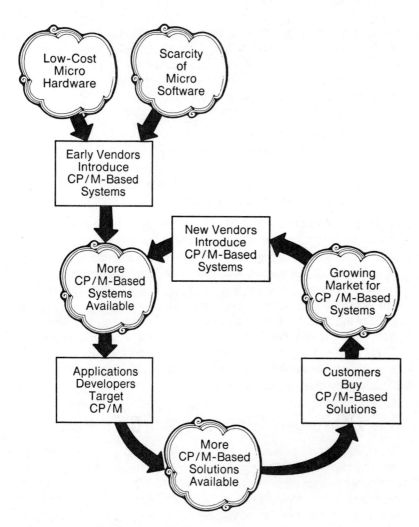

Fig. 2.1. The standardization cycle.

At its announcement the IBM PC was long on hardware and very short on applications software. Three different operating systems were introduced to tap the widest range of existing software:

- *CP/M-86*, a 16-bit revision of CP/M, which offered compatibility with 8-bit CP/M.

- The *UCSD Pascal p-system*, an interactive Pascal inter-preter that offered excellent portability for applications software.
- *MS-DOS*, a brand new operating system written for IBM by Microsoft.

MS-DOS (Microsoft Disk Operating System) was the "sleeper" of the three systems, and on the surface, it appeared the least likely to achieve dominant status. But with IBM's support and encourage-ment of third-party software developers, MS-DOS quickly vaulted into prominence as the standard operating system for the IBM PC. The standardization cycle was set in motion again for single-user 16-bit PCs, with a large helping hand from IBM. Again, the impact was dramatic. Manufacturers rushed to produce MS-DOS-based systems, and software suppliers created hundreds of MS-DOS-based software packages. The resulting PC market was measured in millions of units, compared to the tens of thousands for the earlier generation of 8-bit systems.

XENIX and the 32-Bit Microcomputer

The growing popularity of XENIX and other versions of UNIX is closely linked to the development of the new generation of 16/32-bit microprocessors. Manufacturers such as Altos, Onyx, and Tandy pioneered the introduction of multiuser systems based on these new processors during the early 1980s. These supermicro systems offered computing power comparable to the minicomputers of only a few years before. With this dramatic improvement in hardware ca-pability, computer hardware development again outpaced the in-dustry's ability to develop software for taking advantage of this increased capability. Once again, microcomputer manufacturers found themselves in a market starved for software.

The various versions of UNIX have filled this "supermicro software gap." Because UNIX had been developed for minicomputers, it of-fered the level of sophistication needed to take advantage of the 16/32-bit supermicros. Specifically, UNIX provided multiuser sup-port, excellent software development tools, features to support mcre powerful applications, and a file system capable of organizing and storing data in a multiuser environment. As a result, supermicro manufacturers seized on UNIX as their operating system of choice.

Today, versions of UNIX are offered on more multiuser microcomputer systems than on any other operating system. The standardization cycle experienced by CP/M and MS-DOS is being replayed on 16/32-bit systems, with UNIX in the starring role. Table 2.1 summarizes the relationships among CP/M, MS-DOS, and UNIX in the spectrum of microcomputer hardware.

Word Sizes	8-bit	8/16-bit	16-bit	16/32-bit	32-bit
Micro-processors	• 8080 • Z80	• 8088	• 8086 • Z8000	• 80286 • M68000 • 16032	• 80386 • M68020 • Z80000 • 32032
Operating Systems	CP/M	MS-DOS	UNIX/XENIX		
Systems	Single User		Multiuser		

Table 2.1. Standard Operating Systems

XENIX and the IBM PC AT

Of all the versions of UNIX, XENIX has become the most popular, achieving the largest installed base on low-cost, high-volume supermicros. IBM has reinforced its leadership position with the announcement of XENIX for the PC AT. The PC AT introduction was, in many ways, a replay of the original PC introduction held three years earlier. Again, IBM brought new, advanced technology to the personal computer marketplace. And again, the company announced more than one operating system for its new PC.

Three years earlier, CP/M had been the leader in the established 8-bit market. MS-DOS was an unknown product designed to take advantage of the new 16-bit technology. In 1984 MS-DOS was the leader in the 16-bit PC market, and XENIX was the relative unknown. But MS-DOS is still a single-user operating system, whereas XENIX can fully exploit the multiuser potential of the PC AT and more powerful PCs yet to come. With IBM's support, XENIX *could* achieve the same dominant, industry-standard status for multiuser microcomputer systems that MS-DOS achieved for single-user personal computers.

A Brief UNIX History

For a system whose primary claim to fame is its sophisticated, multiuser features, the UNIX system had very humble origins. It not only began life as a single-user system, but also was a small, relatively unsophisticated piece of software, written for an obscure and long-since-obsolete computer system. Nonetheless, the creation of UNIX was unique in several respects. It was designed and developed by a small group of people with a single purpose in mind: to build a superior environment for software development. Unlike most commercial operating systems, which are developed "by committee" and designed to serve the proprietary needs of hardware manufacturers, UNIX was guided by a consistent vision of its purpose. Its developers also had a commitment to what computer scientists call "elegance"—a combination of simplicity, sophistication, power, and compactness. This guiding philosophy led to the development of an amazingly flexible and capable system.

The history of UNIX began in the late 1960s with a programmer named Ken Thompson, working at Bell Telephone Laboratories in New Jersey. Thompson and others in the Computing Science Research Group were using an early "time-sharing" computer, the General Electric GE 645. It ran an advanced, interactive operating system called Multics, which had been developed at MIT. Though the Multics system was powerful, it also was expensive to use, especially for one of Thompson's programs named Space Travel.

Thompson decided to move the Space Travel program to a dedicated computer system, a Digital Equipment Corporation PDP-7. This system offered a good hardware environment for running Space Travel, but the computer lacked the kind of software support needed to develop programs like Thompson's. UNIX, then, was born out of necessity as a set of software routines to support use of the PDP-7. This first version of the UNIX system, totally written in PDP-7 assembly language, was completed in 1969.

The origin of the name "UNIX" carries its own irony. The name came from Multics, with the *multi*user orientation of that name changed to *uni* to reflect the single-user focus of UNIX. Multiuser versions of UNIX were to come much later, after it had been completely rewritten and transported to different hardware. The single-user version of UNIX became operational in 1971 and apparently caught on well within Bell Labs.

The early history of UNIX is closely intertwined with the development of the C programming language, in which later versions of the operating system were written. The original UNIX system was written in PDP-7 assembly language. A subsequent version incorporated software written in a language called "B," which was developed by Thompson in 1970. The B language was later used to help transport UNIX to the newer PDP-11 family of systems in early 1971. The PDP-11 proved to be an extremely popular minicomputer system, both in the general marketplace and at Bell Labs. Groups within the Labs soon began using their PDP-11s with UNIX software instead of the proprietary DEC operating systems.

The B language caught the eye of Dennis Ritchie, another programmer working at the Labs, who extended and refined the language, calling the result "C." The C language proved to be excellent for implementing systems programs. It combined "structured programming" features, which have proved popular in languages like Pascal, with the ability to "get at the bits and bytes," which is required for efficiency in operating system development. The UNIX system itself was rewritten in C in 1973.

A major reason for rewriting UNIX in C was the desire to move UNIX to a wider range of machines. The first real test of UNIX portability came in mid-1977, with the decision to move UNIX to the Interdata 8/32, a 32-bit computer system very unlike the PDP-11. The Interdata port was successful, and UNIX has since been implemented on a wider range of hardware than that of any other operating system. Today, versions of UNIX are available from AT&T for the PDP-11 and VAX system families from DEC, and for AT&T's own family of computer systems. Software houses and computer manufacturers outside AT&T have ported UNIX to an even broader variety of processors, from systems as small as the IBM PC to the multi-million-dollar Cray-II supercomputer.

Through the early and mid-1970s, UNIX remained primarily a tool for use within the Bell System, and AT&T discouraged outside use through large license fees. Nonetheless, UNIX became popular among researchers doing work for the Department of Defense's Advanced Research Projects Agency (ARPA). Educational institutions were allowed to license UNIX at greatly reduced fees, and many universities took advantage of the opportunity. As a result, colleges became another UNIX stronghold. Today, over 80 percent of colleges granting degrees in computer science are licensed to use the UNIX system, and a computer science student is not likely to complete an undergraduate education without coming into contact with UNIX. Bell's liberal, educational licensing policy has created a large pool of computer science graduates, all familiar with the advantages and capabilities of UNIX as a software development vehicle.

The history of UNIX as a commercially available operating system is a very short one. It began at a company named Onyx Systems, founded in 1978 by Bob Marsh and Kip Myers. The early Onyx systems were multiuser, 8-bit microcomputers, but attention soon turned to the more powerful 16-bit microprocessors. Convinced that 16-bit systems demanded a more powerful operating system than their 8-bit predecessors, Marsh approached AT&T and successfully negotiated the first commercial UNIX license. An Onyx system running UNIX was shown at the National Computer Conference in 1980, much to the amazement of show attendees who couldn't believe that UNIX was actually running on a micro.

UNIX on microcomputers was given a further boost in late 1981, when AT&T announced new licensing provisions. Both royalty rates and the initial source code fee were reduced dramatically, and many licensing restrictions were relaxed. Today, a manufacturer can buy a version of UNIX for a newly introduced system for as little as

$20,000 from a number of software houses who specialize in porting UNIX.

Microsoft and the Development of XENIX

XENIX was introduced in 1980 by Microsoft Corporation, one of the premier suppliers of microcomputer software. Microsoft is best known as the developer of the MS-DOS operating system for the IBM PC and its look-alikes. The company is also known for its line of best-selling applications software for the PC, including Multiplan, Microsoft Word, Microsoft Chart, and others. But the history of Microsoft begins long before the introduction of the PC or the XENIX system, back in the earliest days of the microcomputer industry.

Microsoft was founded in 1975 by Bill Gates and Paul Allen while Gates was still an undergraduate at Harvard University. The two had been childhood friends, and together they became dedicated computer enthusiasts, looking forward to the day when they could afford their own computers. The now-famous issue of *Popular Electronics* appeared in January of 1975, with the MITS Altair computer, a very early 8-bit system, on the cover. Seeing an opportunity, Gates called MITS and claimed that he and his partner had a running BASIC language for the new machine. The two then rushed to develop the product, which did not yet exist, and six weeks later, they demonstrated a working version to MITS. MITS licensed the product, and the royalties that it generated funded the fledgling software company of Gates and Allen, which they named Microsoft.

Over the next several years, Microsoft's M-BASIC became one of the most popular languages for early 8-bit microcomputers. Microsoft later expanded M-BASIC into a full line of computer languages for use with CP/M. In the early 8-bit market, Digital Research was the operating system vendor, and Microsoft was the language supplier.

The roles of the two software companies changed dramatically with the introduction of the IBM PC. IBM first approached Digital Research to create an operating system for the PC, with the intention of licensing only language products from Microsoft. But Digital Research was not responsive to the first IBM overtures, and IBM turned to Microsoft to develop a PC operating system as well. The resulting MS-DOS operating system (called PC DOS by IBM) catapulted Microsoft into position as the largest microcomputer software firm. In an interesting role reversal, Digital Research later became a leading supplier of languages for MS-DOS.

Whereas MS-DOS was developed by Microsoft specifically under contract to IBM, XENIX was developed as a strategic product. As early as the late 1970s, Gates was convinced that the coming generation of 16- and 32-bit microprocessors would demand a more powerful operating system than the CP/M standard of the day. Gates was an early convert to UNIX and believed that it could eventually become a dominant microcomputer operating system. By being the first to offer a version of UNIX suitable for microcomputers, Gates hoped to establish XENIX as a standard.

Microsoft announced XENIX in August of 1980, but first deliveries of the product did not occur until many months later. The early acceptance of XENIX was disappointing. It was almost lost in the wake of the explosive success of MS-DOS and the IBM PC. A few manufacturers, such as Tandy and Altos, pioneered XENIX-based multiuser systems. Their systems sold well but not spectacularly, creating an installed base of about 30,000 XENIX systems by mid-1984.

With the introduction of XENIX on the IBM PC AT, attention has once again turned to the market potential of multiuser microcomputer systems. IBM's introduction has brought multiuser systems into the retail personal computer market and has opened up the opportunity for high-volume sales of XENIX-based systems. This latest chapter in the history of XENIX is still being written and will determine whether XENIX becomes an interesting curiosity or an industry-standard product with the same stature as CP/M and MS-DOS.

Versions of the UNIX System

Many different versions of UNIX are in existence today. AT&T itself licenses several "official" versions. Research at the University of California at Berkeley has produced the popular Berkeley versions of UNIX. Several independent software companies, such as Microsoft, offer enhanced UNIX versions. Hardware vendors routinely modify and extend all these versions in adapting them to their own computer systems. Finally, a few software companies offer UNIX look-alikes, which emulate UNIX but are not based on any of the AT&T versions.

AT&T's licensing policies have contributed to the confusion surrounding versions of UNIX. AT&T licenses the UNIX software but not the UNIX trademark. Software suppliers and computer manufacturers, therefore, cannot name their products "UNIX." Instead, each vendor is forced to call its UNIX version by a unique name: XENIX from Microsoft, Zeus from Zilog, UniPlus+ from UniSoft, etc. This proliferation of names has contributed even more to the apparent diversity of the various UNIX versions. Table 2.2 lists some of the most common versions of UNIX.

AT&T Versions

Over a period of time, AT&T has licensed several successive versions of the UNIX system. Some of these versions were simply revisions of the system, whereas others added specialized features for a particular application. The major versions released by AT&T were the following:

- *Sixth Edition:* the earliest licensed version. Most licensees were educational institutions, and a small number of installations still exist in the academic community. None of the commercial microcomputer ports are based on this version.
- *Seventh Edition (Version 7):* the first version to be commercially licensed by AT&T. Some microcomputer ports are still based on Version 7.
- *PWB/UNIX (Programmer's Workbench):* a specialized version that grew out of software development activity at Bell Labs. This version includes specialized utilities for managing software development by large teams of programmers. PWB/UNIX was initially installed inside Bell in 1973 and was first licensed somewhat later.

AT&T versions:

    Sixth Edition
    Version 7
    PWB/UNIX
    System III
    System V

Versions derived from AT&T versions:

4.1bsd,4.2bsd	UC Berkeley
AUROS	Auragen
CPIX	IBM
FOS	FORTUNE Systems
HP-UX	Hewlett-Packard
IS/1	Interactive Systems
OSx	Pyramid Technology
PERPOS	Computer Consoles
PC/IX	IBM
Sys3	Plexus Computers
UNX/VS	Data General
Ultrix	DEC
UniPlus+	Unisoft
Unisys	Codata
UNITY	Human Computing Resources
UTS	Amdahl
VENIX	VenturCom
XENIX	Microsoft
Zeus	Zilog

Look-alike versions:

Coherent	Mark Williams
Cromix	Cromemco
Idris	Whitesmith
Micronix	Morrow Designs
PNX	Perq Computers
QNX	Quantum Software

Table 2.2 (Continued on next page)

Regulus   Alcyon
uNETix   LanTech Systems
UNOS   Charles River Data Systems

Source: Yates Ventures

Table 2.2. Versions of the UNIX Systems

- *UNIX SYSTEM III:* an update of Version 7, which includes the features of PWB/UNIX. System III was introduced in late 1981 and first shipped on a microcomputer system the following summer.
- *UNIX SYSTEM V:* the latest version, introduced in 1983. It includes performance improvements and enhanced process-to-process communications. AT&T has announced revisions of System V periodically since its first introduction.

The role of AT&T in the UNIX market has changed significantly since the company first began licensing UNIX to the outside world. During most of the 1970s, AT&T licensed UNIX on an "as is" and unsupported basis. With the advent of UNIX System V, AT&T became a full-fledged software supplier, offering support, documentation, training, and other services. AT&T became a hardware vendor as well, with the introduction of its own computers based on UNIX System V in March of 1984.

AT&T now has a vested interest in the success of its own UNIX version. The company has spent millions of dollars promoting System V as *the* UNIX standard. As part of this effort, AT&T has entered into agreements with Intel, Motorola, National Semiconductor, and Zilog to offer standard versions of System V on each vendor's microprocessor family.

Berkeley UNIX

The University of California at Berkeley became a center of UNIX activity in the late 1970s. This effort produced a set of UNIX utilities and a UNIX port known as the *Berkeley Software Distribution* (*4.1bsd* or *4.2bsd*, depending on the version). The Berkeley software includes support for virtual memory on the VAX superminicomputer family, a powerful text editor called **vi**, and a shell especially suited for C programming, called **csh** (the C shell). Research attention also focused on file system performance and UNIX networking.

Berkeley UNIX became very popular not only in academic circles, but also in engineering and scientific applications, where the large address space offered by virtual memory is needed to accommodate large programs. Other UNIX developers have also recognized the value of the so-called "Berkeley enhancements." Both XENIX and AT&T's System V contain the most popular ones.

Microcomputer UNIX Ports

UNIX is available directly from AT&T, Berkeley, and the microprocessor manufacturers only in source code form. To make UNIX available on a particular computer system, the system manufacturer purchases the UNIX source code and *ports* (rewrites and installs) UNIX to its system. In this process UNIX is adapted to work with the particular hardware features and input/output devices of the computer. The vendor also may choose to enhance UNIX or to take advantage of unique hardware features to improve performance.

A hardware vendor may develop its own UNIX port internally, or the vendor may choose to purchase a port from one of several software suppliers who specialize in porting UNIX. These software suppliers typically offer their own enhanced versions. Microsoft, with its XENIX version, is the most notable example. XENIX has been particularly successful on small multiuser systems based on Intel processors. The UniPlus+ version, from UniSoft, is offered on many M68000-based systems, including those from Pixel and Wicat. Human Computing Resources offers its UNITY version, which has experienced some success on the National Semiconductor 16000 processor family.

PC/IX

XENIX is not the first UNIX version offered by IBM for its personal computers. In January, 1984, IBM introduced a version of UNIX for the IBM PC XT. This version was called *Personal Computer Interactive Executive*, or PC/IX. PC/IX, developed under contract for IBM by Interactive Systems Corporation, was derived from AT&T's UNIX System III and features a full-screen editor developed by Interactive. A related version of UNIX, also developed by Interactive and called VM/IX, is offered on IBM's 4300 mainframe series.

PC/IX was originally developed for the PC XT and is now available for the PC AT as well. The product is offered by an IBM division located in Texas. This division is separate from the Entry Systems Division at Boca Raton, which offers XENIX and the personal computer hardware.

UNIX Look-Alikes

Hardware vendors and software suppliers must pay AT&T a license fee ranging from under one hundred dollars to several thousand dollars for each UNIX-based system sold. To avoid these royalty payments, several software suppliers have developed UNIX look-alikes. These systems mimic the external features of UNIX but have been implemented "from scratch" without the benefit of AT&T's UNIX source code. Consequently, the look-alikes can be sold without paying AT&T royalties. Charles River Data Systems' UNOS operating system, the Coherent operating system from Mark Williams Company, and the uNETix operating system from LanTech Systems are three examples.

The key issues for UNIX look-alikes are their completeness and their compatibility with UNIX. UNIX has grown over the years into a huge collection of software (over eight million bytes in System V), and there is a great temptation to "cut corners" when developing a look-alike, implementing only the most commonly used commands or features. But choosing what to leave out is a risky proposition because there is no way to tell in advance which particular commands or features an application program will use. The look-alikes have had limited success, particularly in the face of AT&T's heavy promotion of System V.

The Move to Standardize UNIX

One of the most common criticisms of the UNIX system is the lack of a single, standard version. Unlike CP/M or MS-DOS, each of which is controlled by a single operating system vendor, control of UNIX is spread among AT&T, the hardware vendors, and the UNIX software companies, such as Microsoft.

Several powerful forces are at work trying to establish a standard version of UNIX. AT&T has poured millions of dollars into promotion of UNIX System V. Berkeley UNIX is a *de facto* standard on engineering and scientific systems, such as superminicomputers and CAD/CAM systems. Microsoft is using high-volume distribution and its tie to MS-DOS to promote XENIX as a standard. But because IBM offers UNIX versions based on Version 7, System III, and XENIX, these standardization efforts are disrupted.

A vendor-independent standards effort for UNIX-compatible systems was mounted in 1981 by /usr/group, an association of UNIX users and vendors. The goal was to establish a single standard that would reduce the differences, real and perceived, among the various UNIX versions. Participation in the effort came from the leading UNIX-based hardware manufacturers and software vendors, and even included representation from Bell Labs. The standard (based on UNIX System III) was adopted by /usr/group in 1984. Given the powerful special interests at work in the UNIX marketplace, however, it seems unlikely that this or any other single standard for UNIX will emerge.

3

XENIX, UNIX, and MS-DOS

XENIX is not unchallenged in its status as a new industry-standard operating system. Other versions of UNIX offer alternatives to XENIX, and some of them have achieved considerable success. MS-DOS has also grown in capability to include many of the key features of XENIX. Indeed, networks of PCs based on MS-DOS pose a serious challenge to XENIX-based multiuser systems in some applications. This chapter provides a discussion of the relationship of XENIX to the various versions of UNIX and compares XENIX to MS-DOS.

XENIX and UNIX

XENIX was originally derived from AT&T's UNIX Version 7. More recently, XENIX has been enhanced to include the features of UNIX System III. Microsoft has ported XENIX to all the major 16-bit and 16/32-bit microprocessors, including the Zilog Z8000, the Intel 8086 family, and the Motorola M68000 family. In creating XENIX, Microsoft improved and extended the functions of the AT&T UNIX versions to produce an operating system that was better suited for use on multiuser microcomputer systems. Microsoft's improvements and extensions to UNIX are shown in table 3.1.

• Automatic file system recovery	• Record and file locking
• Bad block handling	• Shared memory
• Performance tuning	• Semaphores
• Documentation	• Nonblocking reads
• Bug fixes	• Synchronous writes

Table 3.1. Microsoft Improvements and Enhancements to UNIX

XENIX Improvements

XENIX includes a number of Microsoft improvements to existing UNIX features, which make XENIX a better commercial multiuser operating system. These improvements include the following:

- *Automatic file system recovery.* XENIX features and utilities permit automatic file system recovery from a system failure, thus simplifying system administration.
- *Bad block handling.* XENIX can be configured to avoid bad spots on a hard disk, either through XENIX software routines or by taking advantage of similar hardware capabilities in the disk controller.
- *Performance tuning.* UNIX was developed for minicomputer environments with relatively large main memories and fast disk drives. XENIX has been performance-tuned for the smaller main memories and slower disks commonly found on microcomputer systems.
- *Documentation.* The UNIX documentation is notoriously cryptic and difficult to use, especially for inexperienced users. The XENIX documentation includes tutorial guides for system use, software development, and text processing, as well as improved reference information.
- *Bug fixes.* XENIX incorporates corrections to known bugs in the AT&T software distributions, as well as numerous bugs discovered through extensive field use of XENIX.

XENIX Enhancements

XENIX also includes several significant Microsoft enhancements to the functions provided in AT&T's UNIX versions. Most of these added features are important to programmers developing turnkey applications and are described in Chapter 8. The enhancements include the following:

- *Record and file locking.* Multiple applications programs can concurrently access a shared file, such as an on-line data base.
- *Shared memory.* Several applications programs can share access to a common portion of main memory for very fast process-to-process communications.
- *Semaphores.* XENIX incorporates a semaphore facility that allows several programs to synchronize their access to a shared resource, such as a system printer.
- *Nonblocking reads.* Under UNIX, read requests normally cause a program to wait indefinitely if the requested data is not yet available. XENIX allows these requests to return immediately, for polling of terminals, communications lines, etc.
- *Synchronous writes.* Programs can selectively "turn off" the XENIX disk buffering scheme for critical files where data integrity must be guaranteed even in the case of system failure. Synchronous writes are described in Chapter 5.

The XENIX Strategy

Microsoft began development of XENIX even before the introduction of its MS-DOS operating system for the IBM PC. The company's strategy was to offer the first commercially viable microcomputer version of UNIX and thus to establish XENIX as an industry standard. This strategy contained four key elements:

- *Availability.* UNIX was available from AT&T only in the form of source code for either the DEC VAX or PDP-11 systems. XENIX, on the other hand, was already configured for the major microprocessors, thus requiring only minor porting effort to a specific computer system.

- *Commercial extensions.* XENIX included several key features that were lacking in the UNIX versions from AT&T. By purchasing XENIX, hardware manufacturers could avoid the work of correcting these deficiencies in their own UNIX versions.
- *Financial leverage.* Royalty payments to AT&T declined with volume under the UNIX licensing agreement. Microsoft could price XENIX very attractively because the volumes from all its XENIX licensees combined to earn larger discounts under a single AT&T contract.
- *Quality control.* UNIX had been developed in a research environment at Bell Labs and had a history of poor documentation, no support, and capricious changes from release to release. XENIX, however, was backed by Microsoft's commitment to support it as a commercial product.

Microsoft's strategy has been somewhat successful, as several major vendors have chosen XENIX as their version of the UNIX operating system. Table 3.2 lists the vendors who offer XENIX.

XENIX versus MS-DOS

A frequently asked question about XENIX is "How does it compare to MS-DOS?" This question is particularly relevant because of the special relationship between the two operating systems. Both are Microsoft products. Both are now available on the same computer system—the IBM PC AT. And each has its future at stake in the confrontation between multiuser systems and personal computer networks.

The comparison between XENIX and MS-DOS is one that is changing with time. The two operating systems have their origins in vastly different computer environments and, as a result, provide very different levels of capability. MS-DOS, however, has slowly but steadily evolved into a much more sophisticated operating system, incorporating many of the major features of XENIX.

Vendor	System
Altos	Altos 586
	Altos 986
Apple	Lisa
Durango	Poppy II
Encore	MPU-8000
General Automation	Zebra 2000
IBM	IBM PC AT
	IBM PC XT
	System 9000
Intel	Intel 286/380
Tandy/Radio Shack	TRS-80 Model 16
Spectrix Microsystems	Spectrix 10
Visual Technology	Visual 2000

Table 3.2. Vendors of XENIX-Based Systems

The Evolution of MS-DOS

At its creation, MS-DOS was defined by the hardware constraints of the IBM PC. The first PCs could be purchased with as little as 64K of main memory and a single floppy disk drive. Compact size and simplicity were therefore the key goals for MS-DOS. Initially, it was little more than a straightforward imitation of CP/M, reimplemented for the 16-bit Intel 8088.

Since then, MS-DOS has grown in sophistication, as the capacity of the PC has expanded and PC users have demanded more capability. XENIX provided the inspiration for much of this growth, and successive revisions of MS-DOS have incorporated many of XENIX's major features, such as its hierarchical file system, input/output redirection, and pipes. Figure 3.1 shows the evolution of these MS-DOS features.

The success of MS-DOS has had an impact on XENIX as well. The user interface of the XENIX visual shell is based on Microsoft's family of MS-DOS applications packages. XENIX utilities support exchange of data between MS-DOS and XENIX applications. XENIX now includes a cross-development environment for creating MS-DOS applications under XENIX. Microsoft has also announced that its Windows package will be offered for both MS-DOS and XENIX.

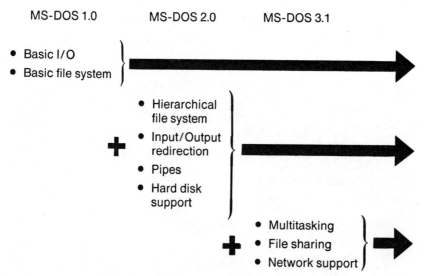

Fig. 3.1. MS-DOS feature evolution.

Comparing XENIX and MS-DOS

On the surface, MS-DOS and XENIX now share a number of popular features. But these similarities mask important underlying differences. MS-DOS continues to be a single-user operating system, designed to harness the power of a personal computer for a single individual. As a multiuser system, XENIX is designed for *sharing* computer power and common data among the users in a work group. Table 3.3 summarizes the fundamental differences between XENIX and MS-DOS.

MS-DOS	XENIX
• Single user	• Multiuser
• Memory-based operation	• Disk-based operation
• Personal data	• Shared access to common data
• Screen-intensive applications	• Disk-intensive applications
• Multitasking for related tasks (TopView)	• Multiprogramming for related and unrelated tasks
• Friendly for end-users	• Friendly for programmers

Table 3.3. A Comparison of MS-DOS and XENIX

XENIX also offers a level of functional capability far surpassing that of MS-DOS. Table 3.4 compares XENIX and MS-DOS (and CP/M for its historical significance), using several different measures of their relative sophistication. The greater size of XENIX and the larger number of commands it offers reflect its greater capability.

An excellent example of this difference in sophistication is found in the XENIX utility **grep**, which searches text files for occurrences of a particular pattern. MS-DOS includes a similar utility, called **FIND**. But the MS-DOS utility allows matching on only a literal string of characters, whereas **grep** supports much more flexible pattern matching. The **grep** utility, for example, can locate lines in a document that contain two words, even if they are separated by one or more intermediate words.

Similar contrasts can be drawn for the other XENIX utilities that have MS-DOS counterparts. Furthermore, many of the XENIX utilities implement functions that are not available under MS-DOS. Examples include most of the XENIX utilities for file processing, text processing, program development, and communications.

Operating system	CP/M-80	MS-DOS 2.0	XENIX
Total System Software	Approx. 100K bytes	Approx. 250K bytes	Over 5M bytes
Resident Operating System Size	8-12K bytes	12-25K bytes	80-200K bytes
System Calls	Approx. 40	Approx. 75	Approx. 60
Commands/ Utilities	Approx. 10	Approx. 30	Over 200
Typical System Price Range	$1,000-$5,000	$3,000-$10,000	$8,000-$50,000

Table 3.4. An Operating System Comparison

Multiuser Systems versus PC Networks

XENIX and MS-DOS present two alternative approaches to meeting the computing requirements of a work group. XENIX is the core of a *multiuser system*, a single computer that is shared among multiple users. MS-DOS provides the software foundation for a *PC network*, in which sharing is accomplished by linking personal computers.

Figure 3.2 illustrates the XENIX approach. Its advantage lies in the natural support XENIX provides for concurrent access to shared data. For applications such as inventory control or order processing, where all users of the system must have the same up-to-the-minute information, this type of access is essential.

The disadvantage of the multiuser approach is the performance degradation the system suffers as more and more users are added to it. The solution is often to buy a larger replacement system, but this kind of growth can be both expensive and disruptive.

The competing MS-DOS approach is illustrated in figure 3.3. The PC network avoids the performance bottlenecks of multiuser systems by giving dedicated processing power to each user. Growth is smooth and modular as more PCs are added to the network, one by one, to support additional users.

PC networks are also better suited for screen-oriented personal applications, such as spreadsheets and word processors. A high percentage of each user's processor can be dedicated to screen I/O, thus making user interaction quite fast.

PC networks offer an imperfect solution to the problem of sharing data, however. Files can be easily exchanged between individual PCs on the network. But coordinating true concurrent access to a

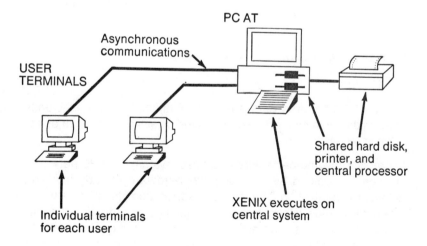

Fig. 3.2. Multiuser systems—the XENIX approach.

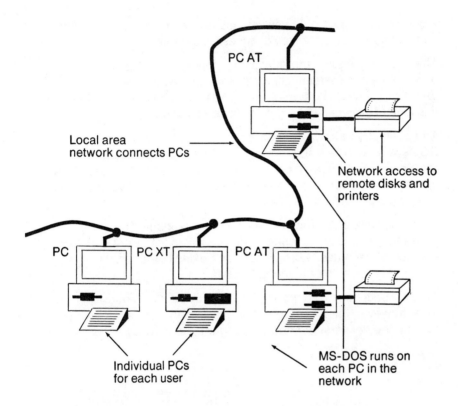

Fig. 3.3. PC networks—the MS-DOS approach.

single copy of shared data is extremely difficult. In fact, efficiently sharing data in a multiprocessor network is still a major area of academic research.

In practice, the choice between multiuser systems and PC networks is often determined by the computer hardware already installed within an organization. The intended application also plays a major role in the choice. When data processing is the predominant application, XENIX-based systems offer the best solution. Installations where personal productivity applications predominate should use the PC network approach. The future will probably see a merger of the two approaches as personal computers are linked to multiuser systems.

4

A Structural Overview

XENIX is a large and complex operating system. The standard XENIX system provides the user with over two hundred different commands for interacting with the system and literally thousands of options to these commands. A few of the commands are used each time a user enters the system. Others are regularly used for specialized functions, such as text processing, communications, or software development. Still other functions, such as accounting and error-checking utilities, are of interest only to system administrators. This chapter describes the overall structure of the XENIX system and provides a brief overview of each major component. The individual components are discussed in greater detail in the following chapters.

A Typical XENIX-Based System

A typical XENIX-based computer system includes a number of hardware and software components. Figure 4.1 shows a multiuser

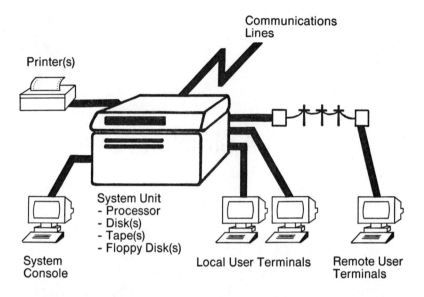

Fig. 4.1. A typical multiuser XENIX-based system.

microcomputer system, representative of those supporting XENIX. The system includes the following hardware components:

- A *system unit*, which houses the system's central processing unit and one or more disk drives for mass storage. The system unit also includes a backup device, such as a floppy disk.
- A *console*, from which system operation is controlled. The system displays error messages on the console. It is often used as an ordinary user terminal as well. On the PC AT the console is the system's main keyboard and display.
- *User terminals*, at which users interact with the system, typing commands on the keyboard and receiving output on the display. XENIX supports user terminals that are directly attached to the computer system, as well as those that are connected to the system by communications lines and modems. The PC AT supports up to two user terminals; other XENIX-based supermicro systems support as many as ten or more.

- *Communications lines*, connecting the system to other XENIX-based systems.
- *Printers*, used to obtain hard copy output. XENIX supports draft-quality printers, letter-quality printers, and even phototypesetters.

The Structure of XENIX

Figure 4.2 shows the major software components that make up the XENIX system and their interrelationships. The major components are the following:

- The *kernel* is the core of the XENIX system, controlling the system hardware and performing various low-level functions. The other parts of the XENIX system, as well as user programs, call on the kernel to perform services for them.

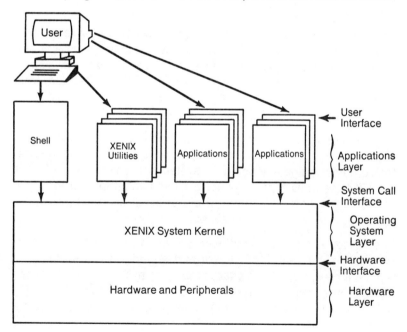

Fig. 4.2. The structure of XENIX.

- The *shell* is the command interpreter for the XENIX system. The shell accepts user commands and is responsible for seeing that they are carried out. XENIX offers a choice of several alternative shells.
- Over two hundred *utility programs* are supplied with the XENIX system. These utilities (or commands) support a variety of tasks, such as copying files, editing text, performing calculations, and developing software.
- *User programs* can be developed, using the XENIX utilities, or purchased "off the shelf" from software suppliers. These programs occupy the same logical position within the XENIX system structure as that of the XENIX utilities. In fact, once installed on a XENIX system, user programs and XENIX commands are indistinguishable.

The XENIX Kernel

The core of the XENIX system is the kernel, which performs the low-level functions that create the "XENIX environment" on a particular computer system. The kernel interacts directly with the system hardware and insulates the other parts of the XENIX system from hardware dependencies. XENIX utilities and user programs call on the kernel to perform services for them.

The functions performed by the kernel and the services it provides are shown in figure 4.3. The kernel implements the XENIX file system, organizing and managing the system's mass storage; enforces the XENIX security scheme, which prevents unauthorized access to stored information; and performs input and output on request, transferring data to and from I/O devices.

The kernel also polices multiuser operation of the XENIX system, scheduling the central processor and ensuring that work is performed for each user who shares the system. The kernel manages the system's main memory, allocating it among the user tasks. Finally, the kernel maintains accounting logs, recording both system activity and usage.

At the lowest level, the kernel communicates directly with the hardware. Parts of the kernel, therefore, must be custom-tailored to each particular computer system's hardware features. For example, each

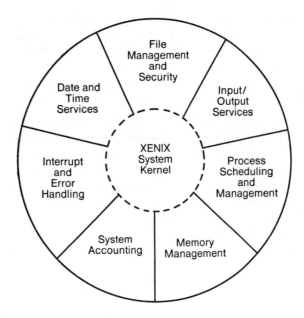

Fig. 4.3. Functions of the XENIX kernel.

system manages its main memory somewhat differently, and the memory management software in the kernel must be changed to accommodate these differences. Each system also includes I/O devices with slightly different hardware characteristics. The parts of the kernel that deal directly with I/O devices—such as video screens, printers, and disk drives— are called *drivers,* and these drivers must also be adapted to each new system. *Porting* a XENIX system is the process of adapting the hardware-dependent pieces of the kernel.

The System Call Interface

XENIX utilities and applications programs call on the kernel to perform services for them. The mechanism used to request kernel services is called a *system call.* Each system call instructs the kernel to perform one particular service on behalf of the program making the call. For example, each time an application program wants to read a line of user input from a terminal, the program calls the kernel, which obtains the requested data and passes it on to the program. System calls are the interface between XENIX-based applications programs and the XENIX kernel; these calls are the only way that applications programs and the kernel interact directly in a XENIX-based system. Figure 4.4 illustrates the operation of a XENIX system call.

The XENIX kernel supports over sixty different system calls. *These calls are identical on every XENIX system.* No matter what hardware differences exist "down below," or whether the system is an IBM PC AT or another multiuser supermicro, the system calls are the same. Thus, the system calls form a standard interface for the XENIX system. Applications programs using only the standard system calls operate in the same way on every XENIX-based system, without modification to the programs. In addition, the XENIX system calls are highly compatible with the system calls found in other versions of UNIX. The commonality of the system call interface gives XENIX its vendor independence.

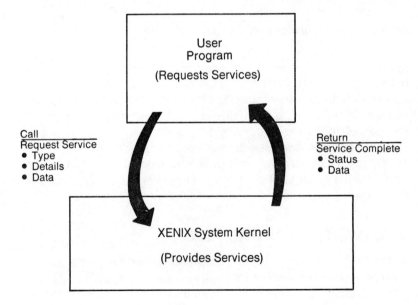

Fig. 4.4. Anatomy of a system call.

The power and flexibility of the XENIX system calls make the kernel a powerful base for executing user-developed and off-the-shelf applications programs. In a real sense, the kernel's system call interface *is* the XENIX system. The particular programs that ride above the kernel specialize XENIX for one particular application or another, but it is the kernel that provides the vendor-independent power which makes XENIX and UNIX a market force.

The Shell

In the XENIX system the shell is the component that interacts directly with the user. The shell is a command interpreter. It accepts commands from the user and causes them to be carried out, one by one. In addition, a number of convenience features provided by the shell make command entry easier and give the user more flexibility in controlling XENIX operation. Chapter 6 describes the XENIX shells in detail.

The XENIX Utilities

The XENIX utilities are a collection of over two hundred programs that are supplied with the XENIX system for performing particular functions. These utilities are the XENIX *commands*, which are invoked, by name, through the shell.

The utilities can be divided, by function, into the following groups:

- General system operation
- File management
- Text processing
- Office support
- Software development
- Communications

The utilities in each group are described in Chapters 5 through 12.

Recall that the kernel by itself offers only a set of low-level services for performing simple functions. Organizing these services into a set of useful user-level functions is the role of XENIX utilities.

Unfortunately, as utilities have been developed and added to the UNIX system over the years, they have been given short names that only vaguely describe their functions. Consequently, the commands are easy to type, which saves keystrokes, but also difficult to remember and understand. For this reason, XENIX is sometimes criticized as an "unfriendly" system.

5
The File System

One of the most powerful and attractive features of XENIX is the file system, which manages data stored on the computer's mass storage devices. The file system's facilities make it easy to organize stored information in a natural way and to retrieve and modify the information, as necessary. Many of the file system's features were unique when UNIX was first created, and they have been so popular that they have since been duplicated in other commercial operating systems. This chapter provides a detailed discussion of the file system's capabilities.

File System Features and Benefits

The XENIX file system includes the following major features:

- *Hierarchical structure*. Users can group together related information and efficiently manipulate a group of files as a unit. The resulting organization resembles the operation of manual filing systems.

- *File expansion.* Files grow dynamically, as needed, taking up only the amount of mass storage space required to store their current contents. The user is not forced to decide in advance how large a file will grow.
- *Structureless files.* XENIX imposes no internal structure on a file's contents. The user is free to structure and interpret the contents of a file in whatever way is appropriate.
- *Security.* Files can be protected against unauthorized use by different users of the XENIX system.
- *File and device independence.* XENIX treats files and input/output devices identically. The same procedures and programs used to process information stored in files can be used to read data from a terminal, print it on a printer, or pass it to another program.

The Concept of a File

The fundamental structure that XENIX uses to store information is the *file*. XENIX files have much in common with the file folders used every day In business. Like file folders, XENIX files store diverse kinds of information. A file can store payroll data, word-processing documents, programming instructions that tell the system how to execute daily procedures, and even excerpts from the XENIX documentation. In short, XENIX files are the structure used to store virtually every kind of information required for the operation of a typical XENIX system.

XENIX keeps track of files internally by assigning each one a unique identifying number. Thus, a customer file may be stored in file number 2217, inventory transactions may be stored in file number 456, and so on. On a typical multiuser XENIX system, it is not unusual to have hundreds of files existing at any one time.

Obviously, identifying files by number can be very tedious; and in practice, file numbers, called *inode numbers*, are used only within the XENIX system itself. Instead of requiring file numbers of users, the file system allows them to identify each file by a user-assigned name. A *file name* can be any sequence containing from one to fourteen characters—usually more than enough to describe meaningfully the file's contents. But even this method poses a problem for a multiuser system with hundreds of files. For example, how can a user be certain, when assigning a name to a new file, that the name selected has not been used previously by some other user?

The Concept of a Directory

XENIX provides users a way of organizing files by grouping them into directories. A *directory* performs the same function as a file drawer in a filing cabinet, gathering together related files in a common place where they can be found easily.

With directories, the user has complete flexibility in grouping files in a meaningful way. For example, a business might maintain files of information on sales results, customer orders, forecasts, and personnel—for each of its sales offices. A sensible way to organize this information is to create a directory for each sales office, with each directory containing only those files that relate to that particular office.

XENIX directories themselves have names, each of which may also contain up to fourteen characters. Again, names describing the kinds of files in the directory are usually chosen. For example, the files for the Boston sales office might be called **results**, **orders**, **forecast**, and **personnel**. The directory containing these files might then be called **boston**. Another common use of directories is to give one to each user, with the directory's name being that of the user. The user's files are then identified through the user's own directory, thus eliminating any confusion with the files of others.

Internally, a directory is just a special file containing a list of file names and their corresponding inode numbers. The directory performs exactly the same function as a common telephone directory. Given the name of a file, XENIX looks in the directory and obtains the corresponding inode number for the file. With this number, the file system can examine other internal tables to determine where the file is stored and to make it accessible to the user. Figure 5.1 shows how directories are used to locate files.

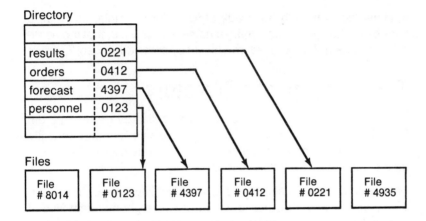

Fig. 5.1. A XENIX directory.

Files with Several Names

A file name is simply a means to identify a file to the XENIX system. In fact, one file may be identified by two or more names! A single file may also be identified in more than one directory. XENIX calls this "having multiple links to a file," because a user can identify the file in more than one way. Multiple links can be useful when more than one user needs access to a file. For example, a sales report may be of interest to several different managers in a company. Without duplicating the file's contents, each manager may call the file by the manager's own name and identify the file through that manager's private directory. Figure 5.2 shows such an arrangement.

Hierarchical File Systems

If grouping files together in directories is a good idea, then why not provide users with the ability to group together directories as well, giving users even more power to organize stored information? For example, because the sales data is organized into directories by sales office, why not group the directories together by sales region to reflect the organization of the sales force?

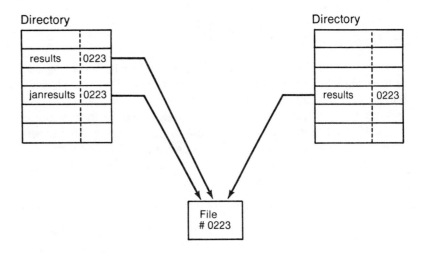

Fig. 5.2. A file with multiple links.

In fact, XENIX allows users to create just such an organization, known as a *hierarchical file system*. At the very top of a hierarchy is a directory. It may contain the names of individual files and the names of other directories. These, in turn, may contain the names of individual files and the names of still other directories, and so on. A hierarchy of files is the result.

The XENIX file hierarchy resembles an upside-down tree, with its root at the top. The various directories branch out until they finally trace a path to the individual files, which correspond to the tree's leaves. You will often hear the XENIX file system described as "tree-structured," with the single directory at the very top of the hierarchy called the *root directory*. The name of the root directory is */*. All the files that can be reached by tracing a path down through the directory hierarchy from the root directory are called a *file system*.

Figure 5.3 shows a file system that might be used for a sales organization. Files for each sales office are grouped into a directory for each office, and these directories are, in turn, grouped by sales region. An additional directory stores programs used to process the data in the sales office files. All the directories relating to the application are grouped under the single directory **sales**.

Path Names

A typical XENIX file system will have many levels in its hierarchy; ten levels from top to bottom are not uncommon. Each file in the file system may be uniquely identified by giving its path name. A *path name* is nothing more than a list of the directories, by name, that lie along the path from the root to the individual file, followed by the file's own name. By convention, the names in a path name are separated by slashes, and the path name begins with a slash to indicate that the name starts at the root directory.[1] Thus, the name

/sales/east/boston/forecast

is the path name for one of the files in figure 5.3. Path names that trace a complete path down from the root directory are called *fully qualified* path names because they describe the complete path that XENIX must take to locate the file.

Partial Path Names

Identifying each file by its full path name can be very cumbersome. In practice, most users work with only a small set of files at one time. Often these files will be grouped together in a single directory. XENIX allows the user to designate this directory as the user's *current working directory.*

For convenience, users can use a shorthand notation, known as a *partially qualified* path name, to identify a file whose path name includes the current working directory. This path name simply omits the initial slash and the directory names up to and including the current working directory. In figure 5.3, if the current working directory is **/sales/east**, then the partially qualified path name of

boston/forecast

identifies the same file as the one identified with a fully qualified path name in the earlier example.

---

[1]Note the confusing dual use of the **/** character: to separate file and directory names from each other within a path name and to serve as the name of the root directory.

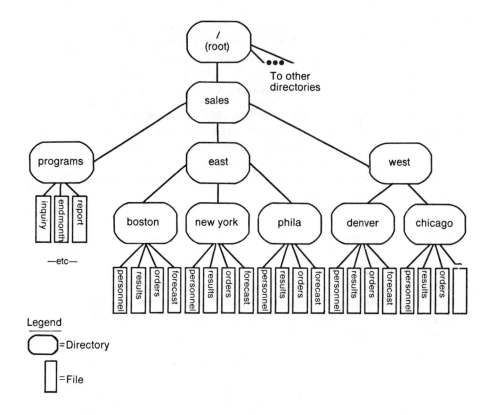

Fig. 5.3. A XENIX file system.

File Information

XENIX maintains a great deal of information about the files it manages. For each file, the file system keeps track of the following:

- Location — Where is the file stored on the disk?
- Size — How large is the file?
- Link count — By how many names is the file known?
- Ownership — Which user "owns" the file?

- Security   Which users may access the file?
- Type   Is the file a directory or not?
- Creation   When was the file created?
- Modification   When was the file last modified?
- Access   When was the file last accessed?

All this information is maintained automatically by the file system as the files are created and used. The information is used by several utilities to process files selectively. For example, the XENIX backup utilities can save copies of only those files that were modified since some specified past date. The time of the last modification is used to select the appropriate files.

Multiple Disks

Most XENIX-based computer systems have at least one permanent, nonremovable hard disk as their principal mass storage. The files stored on this disk are always accessible by the system. The root directory and the file system below it are stored on this disk. This file system is called the *root file system*.

Most XENIX-based computers also support additional hard disks, allowing expansion of the system's mass storage capacity. XENIX manages the files on these disks by creating a separate file system on each hard disk. In other words, each disk has its own complete hierarchical file system, with its own root. The file system on each disk is independent of those on other disks.

Before the file system on an additional hard disk can be used, the file system must first be made accessible to XENIX. This is done by attaching the file system to the root file system, making the attached file system part of the root directory hierarchy. Figure 5.4 illustrates this process of *mounting* a file system. Once the file system has been mounted, its files are accessible as if they were a permanent part of the root file system. Path names for files on the mounted file system begin at the root of the root file system and then branch down through the mounted file system to locate the file.

The process of mounting a file system can be reversed by *unmounting* it, that is, severing its connection to the root. Mounting and unmounting file systems are accomplished through XENIX utility

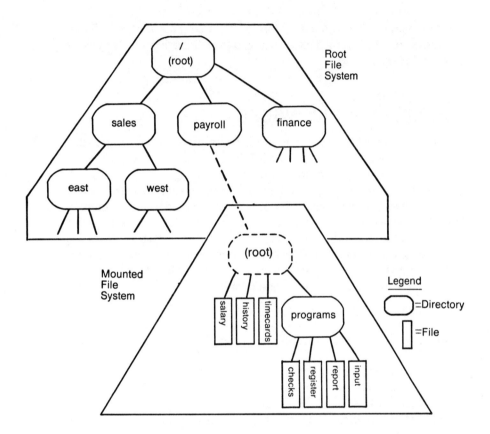

Fig. 5.4. A mounted file system.

commands. Generally, file systems are mounted as part of the XENIX system start-up sequence and are not unmounted until the system shuts down; users, therefore, perceive these file systems as a permanent part of the file hierarchy.

XENIX also allows a single hard disk to be divided into several independent file systems, which can be separately mounted and unmounted. This technique is useful in tuning the performance of a XENIX system or sheltering private data from unauthorized access.

Mountable file systems are also used to organize files on floppy disks. When a floppy disk is inserted into a disk drive, the user must first mount the floppy's file system before using the files in it. Similarly, before the floppy disk is removed from the drive, its file system must be unmounted.

Input/Output Devices

Printers, terminals, and many other types of input and output devices can all be connected to a XENIX system. The file system extends the concept of a file to include all these devices. They are treated as *special files*, which are accessed as if they were simply ordinary files on the system. By convention, all the I/O devices on a XENIX system are given individual file names and grouped together in a directory named **/dev** (short for devices). By tradition, standard names are assigned to the most common devices, as listed in table 5.1. Most XENIX utilities and off-the-shelf applications programs assume that the devices have these names.

File and Device Independence

Input and output operations to I/O devices work just as they do for ordinary files. Applications programs designed to work with files can thus work with all types of I/O devices, with no changes needed. This feature is known as *file and device independence*.

The benefit of treating I/O devices as ordinary files can be simply illustrated. The following XENIX command is used to copy a file named **orders** to a file named **results**:

cp orders results

The same command can be used to "copy" the file to the printer:

cp orders /dev/lp

File and device independence allows a single utility program to be used for many different functions. On operating systems that do not provide this feature, each of these functions must be handled by a separate utility program, adding to the complexity of the system and making the functions more difficult to learn. Figure 5.5 illustrates the file and device independence provided by the XENIX file system.

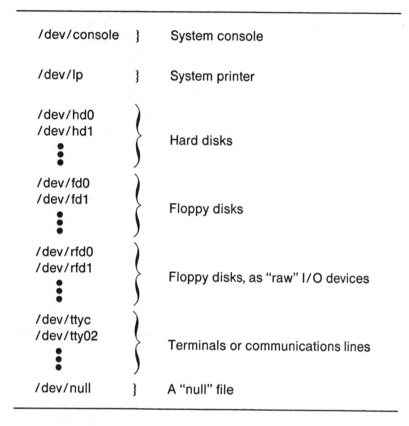

/dev/console   }   System console

/dev/lp   }   System printer

/dev/hd0
/dev/hd1
⋮   Hard disks

/dev/fd0
/dev/fd1
⋮   Floppy disks

/dev/rfd0
/dev/rfd1
⋮   Floppy disks, as "raw" I/O devices

/dev/ttyc
/dev/tty02
⋮   Terminals or communications lines

/dev/null   }   A "null" file

Table 5.1. Typical XENIX System Device Names

The Standard File Hierarchy

XENIX uses its hierarchical file system to organize its own system files. Individual directories are used to store the various components of the XENIX system. For example, the directory **/bin** (short for binary object files) stores the XENIX utilities. The **/etc** directory stores miscellaneous administrative utilities and information, such as the file listing authorized users of the system. The **/tmp** directory stores

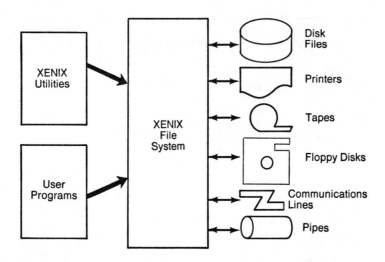

Fig. 5.5. File and device independence.

temporary files. The kernel itself is stored in the file named **/xenix**. Table 5.2 lists the directories typically used to store the component parts of the XENIX system.

In many XENIX systems, each user is given a directory, where all the user's private files and directories are stored. These user directories are often set up as subdirectories of a directory named **/usr**. Thus, Sam's files will appear in the directory **/usr/sam**, and Mary's files, in the directory **/usr/mary**. Figure 5.6 shows these user directories and their relationship to the system directories listed in table 5.2.

File Management Utilities

Several XENIX utilities are tools for managing files and the information they contain. There are utilities for creating new files and directories, for removing unused files from the system, for copying files, and so on. Table 5.3 lists the most frequently used file management utilities.

The command descriptions that follow include examples of typical command use. For each example the user's current working direc-

/bin	XENIX utilities
/dev	Special files (I/O devices)
/etc	Administrative programs and tables
/lib	Libraries used by the XENIX language processors
/tmp	Temporary files
/usr/bin	XENIX utilities (overflow for **/bin**)
/usr/adm	Administrative commands and files
/usr/include	Include files used by the XENIX language processors
/usr/lib	Archive libraries, text-processing macros
/usr/spool	Spool files for printing and XENIX mail files
/usr/tmp	Temporary files

Table 5.2. Directories Used by the XENIX System

tory is **/sales/east/boston,** and the file system shown in figure 5.3 applies.

Identifying the Current Working Directory

The **pwd** (**p**rint **w**orking **d**irectory) utility displays the fully qualified path name of the current working directory:

```
$ pwd
/sales/east/boston
$ ■
```

pwd	Prints the name of the current working directory
cd	Changes the current working directory
ls	Lists the contents of directories
lc	Lists in columns the contents of directories
cat	Concatenates files
mv	Moves and renames files
ln	Creates a new link (name) for a file
cp	Copies files
copy	Copies groups of files or entire file systems
mkdir	Creates new directories
rm	Removes files
rmdir	Removes directories
du	Displays disk usage
quot	Displays disk usage on a per-user basis
df	Displays the number of free blocks for mounted file systems
touch	Updates the time of last modification for files
find	Locates files that match certain criteria

Table 5.3. File Management Utilities

The **pwd** utility is one of the simplest XENIX utilities. It has no options, takes no input, and produces a single line of output.

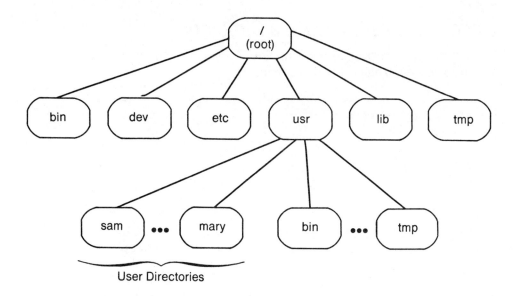

Fig. 5.6. Standard XENIX file hierarchy.

Moving to a Different Current Working Directory

The **cd** (**c**hange working **d**irectory) utility moves the user into a different working directory. For example, if files for the New York sales office are to be used heavily for the next few commands, the command

```
$ cd /sales/east/newyork
$ ■
```

makes **newyork** the current working directory. The New York files can now be conveniently accessed with partially qualified path names.

Listing the File Names in a Directory

The **ls** (**list**) utility lists the files in a directory. For example, to list the files in **/sales/east/phila**, type this command:

```
$ ls /sales/east/phila
forecast
orders
personnel
results
$ ■
```

Omitting the directory name in the command gives a listing of the files in the current working directory. The **ls** command has many options that are used to display different information about the files, such as the date and time of last access and modification, whether the file is an ordinary file or a directory, and so on. One of the most often used options is the so-called "long" option, which produces a very detailed but hard-to-read output, illustrated in figure 5.7.

Viewing File Contents

The **cat** (con**cat**enate files) command is often used to view the contents of a file on a terminal screen. As the name suggests, **cat** is a general-purpose utility, which is more fully described in Chapter 9. Displaying file contents, however, is probably this utility's most frequent use. The file names specified in the command are displayed in sequence on the screen, as in the following example:

```
$ cat personnel
John R. Jones      District Mgr.   1200000   1036000    86%
Paul N. Davis      Salesman        1000000    856730    83%
Mike E. Smith      Salesman         900000   1034360   115%
James R. Harris    Salesman         850000    674390    79%
Dan A. Andrews     Salesman         800000    850340   106%
$ ■
```

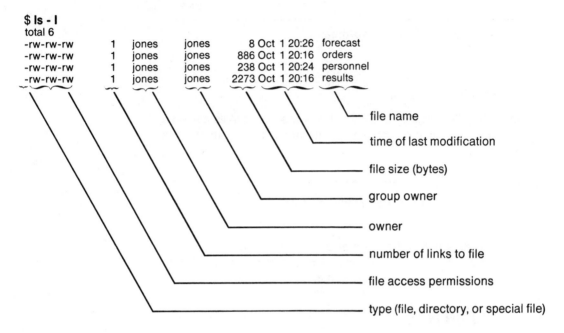

```
$ ls - l
total 6
-rw-rw-rw    1    jones    jones       8 Oct 1 20:26  forecast
-rw-rw-rw    1    jones    jones     886 Oct 1 20:16  orders
-rw-rw-rw    1    jones    jones     238 Oct 1 20:24  personnel
-rw-rw-rw    1    jones    jones    2273 Oct 1 20:16  results
```

file name
time of last modification
file size (bytes)
group owner
owner
number of links to file
file access permissions
type (file, directory, or special file)

*Fig. 5.7. File information from the **ls** command.*

Note that the **cat** utility displays the entire file, line by line, without pause. An alternative utility, called **more**, from the Berkeley UNIX system, is also included in XENIX. This utility pauses after displaying a screenful of data, allowing page-by-page browsing through a file.

Renaming Files

The **mv (move)** utility changes the name of a file. Both the old and the new names for the file are given with this command:

```
$ mv forecast prediction
$ ■
```

In this example the name of a file is changed from **forecast** to **prediction**. The **mv** utility can rename directories in the same way. The command

```
$ mv /sales/east /sales/northeast
$ ▪
```

is used to rename the eastern sales region's directory if the name of the sales territory is changed.

Some kinds of "renaming" of a file actually result in a file's having a different position in the file system hierarchy. For example, the command

```
$ mv forecast /sales/east/newyork/forecast
$ ▪
```

"moves" the **forecast** file from the **boston** directory to the **newyork** directory. In effect, renaming the file has moved it to a new directory. The name of the command suggests this possible use.

Linking File Names

Recall that a file may be known in the XENIX system by several different names. The **ln (link)** command is used to give a file additional names. Both the current name and the new name are given with the following command:

```
$ ln /sales/east/newyork/forecast fantasy
$ ▪
```

The New York **forecast** file is now also identified as **fantasy**. There is still only one copy of the file.

Copying Files

The **cp (copy)** utility makes a duplicate copy of a file. For example, the command

```
$ cp forecast oldforecast
$ ▪
```

duplicates the contents of the **forecast** file and calls it **oldforecast**. Two separate files result, and changes made to one of the files do not affect the other copy of the data.

Making New Directories

The **mkdir** (**make dir**ectory) utility creates a new directory. For example, the command

```
$ mkdir /sales/east/atlanta
$ ▪
```

might be used to make a directory for a new sales office in Atlanta. The newly created directory is *empty;* that is, it contains no files.

Removing File Names

The **rm** (**remove**) command removes unwanted file names from the directory, as in the following:

```
$ rm fantasy
$ ▪
```

If the file to be removed is known by more than one name, only the specified name for the file is removed; the other names and the data itself remain. (In this example the name **fantasy** is removed.) The contents of a file are actually erased from the system only when the last name identifying the file is removed.

To prevent a major accident, the **rm** utility will not ordinarily remove directories. However, an option is available that will delete a directory, as well as all the files and subdirectories it contains. Thus, the command

```
$ rm -r /sales/west
$ ▪
```

removes all the files and directories for the western sales region, including the directory **west** itself.

Removing Directories

The **rmdir** (**r**emove **dir**ectory) utility removes directories that are no longer needed. The name of the directory to be removed is given in the following command:

```
$ rmdir /sales/east/atlanta
$ ▮
```

As a safeguard, the **rmdir** utility will only remove directories that are empty.

Internal File Structure*

Unlike most operating systems, XENIX does not impose a rigid internal structure on the contents of files. In fact, XENIX cares very little about the internal organization of files and provides only one file organization. All XENIX files are treated as a simple sequence of bytes (characters), beginning with the first byte in the file and ending with the last one. An individual byte within the file is identified by its position, relative to the beginning of the file, as shown in figure 5.8.

Most other microcomputer operating systems force users to organize files into *records* or *blocks* of one fixed length. This requirement corresponds to the way that data is organized on the disk. These structures frequently hamper, rather than enhance, the development of applications software. Early versions of MS-DOS, for example, used blocks of 512 bytes. But a report file may naturally be organized as a sequence of 80-character lines, a customer file may contain a two-thousand-character record for each customer, and a document may contain a sequence of paragraphs that vary in length. Programs accessing these files must translate their requirements for accessing lines, records, and paragraphs into requests for one or more blocks from the disk. This method prevents programs from organizing the data in the most natural way for the application.

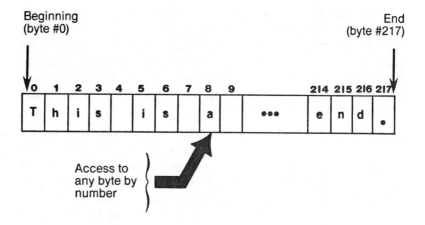

Fig. 5.8. Internal XENIX file organization.

XENIX specifically shields the user from the concept of records or blocks. Instead, XENIX can deliver, on request, a particular byte or sequence of bytes from anywhere in the file. Programs are thus free to organize their files independently of the way the data is actually stored on the disk. The simple internal structure of XENIX files makes access to their contents very simple, too. Information needed from a file is identified by giving its starting position in the file and the length of the data needed. Similarly, information can be placed into a file in any position, again by giving the starting position in the file where the data is to be placed and its length.

Disk Storage Allocation*

The XENIX file system uses advanced techniques for managing disk storage. As information is added to files, XENIX allows them to grow dynamically. The maximum size of a XENIX file is quite large—in excess of two billion bytes. However, unlike operating systems that force users to reserve space in advance for the maximum size a file may achieve, XENIX allows files to take up only as much space as they actually need. When a file is deleted, its disk space is made available to store other files.

XENIX organizes a hard disk as a sequence of 1,024-byte *blocks* (512-byte blocks for floppy disks). The contents of a file are stored in one or more blocks, which may be widely scattered on the disk. A list of the locations of the first ten blocks of a file is stored in the file's *inode*, along with other critical information. The inode is generally available in main memory; therefore, data in the first ten blocks of a file requires only one disk access for retrieval. XENIX thus maximizes the efficiency of processing short files, somewhat at the expense of processing long ones.

If a file is longer than ten blocks, XENIX begins to use "indirect access" techniques. The locations of subsequent blocks of the file are stored, not in the inode, but in another disk block, called an *indirect block*. The location of the indirect block is stored in the inode. Thus, access to data in the eleventh block of a file requires two disk accesses—one to retrieve the indirect block and one to retrieve the actual data block. This *single-indirect* access suffices for most commonly encountered files. Figure 5.9 shows how indirect file access works.

Of course, the indirect block itself can hold only a limited number of block locations, and eventually its capacity is also exhausted. XENIX handles files beyond this limit with a *double-indirect* method. Stored in the inode is the location of one double-indirect block, which contains the locations of many single-indirect blocks. The single-indirect blocks, in turn, contain the locations of blocks of the file. Double indirection requires three disk accesses for every file access. This method suffices for large files.

XENIX permits one more level of indirection, known as *triple-indirect* access, for handling very large files (up to two billion bytes). Another layer is simply added to the scheme, with the location of a triple-indirect block stored in the inode. This block contains the location of double indirect blocks, which contain the locations of single-indirect blocks, and so on.

Disk Buffering*

On many microcomputer systems, input and output to disk files are actually performed at the time these activities are requested by an application program. That is, each request to read data from a file or to write data into a file produces actual disk I/O activity. Although this technique may offer adequate performance for simple personal

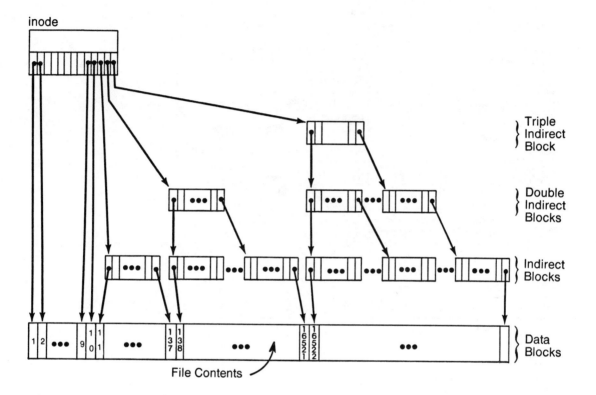

Fig. 5.9. XENIX file access.

computer applications, the technique quickly leads to performance problems under the heavy disk I/O load of a typical multiuser XENIX system.

To minimize the amount of disk I/O actually performed, the XENIX file system uses a sophisticated technique, called *disk buffering*. With this technique some of the blocks of data from the disk are duplicated in main memory by XENIX. A typical multiuser system may have as many as 32 or even 64 disk blocks duplicated in these *disk buffers*.

Figure 5.10 shows how disk buffering works. When a user program tries to read data from the disk, the file system first checks the disk

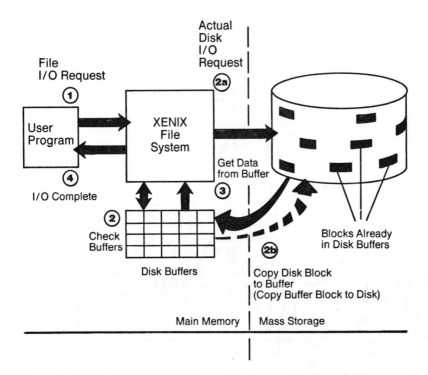

Fig. 5.10. XENIX file system buffering.

buffers to see whether the required disk block is already present there. If it is, the read request can be satisfied without actual disk activity. Similarly, if the program is updating data on the disk, and the corresponding disk block is in one of the disk buffers, XENIX simply modifies the data in the buffer. The contents of the disk buffer will actually be written onto the disk at a later time.

The file system automatically manages the disk buffers. When a user program requires a block of data that is not in one of the disk buffers, the file system decides which of the blocks currently in the buffers will be replaced by the new block. If the block to be replaced has been modified while in the buffer, that block must first be copied to the disk before the new block can be brought in the place of the modified block.

These techniques eliminate many disk I/O operations. Only the first request to read a disk block results in actual disk activity. The information for subsequent reads comes from the buffer. Similarly, repeated requests to write a disk block will only modify the copy of the block in the buffers. An actual disk write occurs only when a modified block of data in the disk buffers is finally replaced. Buffering improves system performance because user programs tend to access the same disk blocks over and over again. The majority of disk I/O requests, therefore, do not result in actual disk I/O.

Synchronous Writes*

Although disk buffering improves the performance of a XENIX system, buffering can also produce data integrity problems. If the data in a disk buffer is updated, and a system failure occurs before the buffer is actually written to the disk, the updated information will be lost. Recovery from such a problem is usually straightforward, since the lost data can often be identified and reentered into the system. But for certain key files (for example, a log of transactions in a transaction-processing application), the integrity of the data on disk *must* be guaranteed at all times.

XENIX solves this data integrity problem through its *synchronous write* facility. When synchronous writes are used, data written to a file is not held in the disk buffers. Instead, the data is immediately written to the disk. In this way, the program writing the data is guaranteed that each disk write request actually updates the data on the disk. In the event of a system failure, the disk always contains current data, thus assuring the integrity of the information stored there.

Synchronous writes can degrade the performance of a XENIX system because they eliminate the performance gains produced by disk buffering. For this reason, synchronous writes are typically used for key files only, such as on-line data bases where reconstructing data would be difficult or impossible. A program must explicitly request synchronous write operation when a disk file is first opened.

6
The Shell

The shell is the most frequently used utility program on a standard XENIX system. XENIX places a user in conversation with the shell at the beginning of each work session with the computer. The user interacts with the shell repeatedly during the session, giving it commands that direct the work of the system on the user's behalf. When the work session is completed, the shell controls termination of the session.

The shell is a sophisticated XENIX utility program. It is the XENIX system's *command interpreter*. The role of the shell is very simple: it accepts commands from the user and causes the XENIX system to obey them. Interacting with the user through the keyboard and the terminal display, the shell manages the dialog between the computer user and the XENIX system. For this reason, the shell is known as the primary *user interface* to the XENIX system.

XENIX actually offers the user the choice of three alternative shells:

- The *Bourne shell*, named after its creator, is the traditional UNIX shell. It is the most commonly used of the three and is presented in the greatest detail in this chapter.

- The *C shell* was originally offered as part of the Berkeley UNIX system. This shell is a particular favorite among programmers because its command structure resembles that of the C programming language. The C shell is described at the end of this chapter.
- The *visual shell*, an end-user-oriented shell developed by Microsoft, is unique to XENIX. This shell offers a full-screen, menu-driven user interface patterned after Multiplan. The visual shell is described at the end of this chapter.

This choice of shells provides XENIX with ease-of-use features for users with varying levels of sophistication. In a typical end-user installation, the visual shell minimizes user training through simple menu choices. The command-driven approach of the Bourne shell and the C shell gives more experienced users an efficient and powerful way of controlling the system.

Bourne Shell Features and Benefits

The Bourne shell includes the following major features:

- *Interactive processing.* Communication between the user and the XENIX system takes the form of an interactive dialog with the shell.
- *Background processing.* Time-consuming, noninteractive tasks can proceed while the user continues with other interactive processing. The system can perform many different tasks at the same time on behalf of a single user.
- *Input/output redirection.* Programs designed to interact with a user at a terminal can easily be instructed to take their input from another source, such as a file, and send their output to another destination, such as a printer.
- *Pipes.* Programs that perform simple functions can easily be connected to perform more complex functions, minimizing the need to develop new programs.
- *Wild-card matching.* The user can specify a pattern to select one or more files as a group for processing. Common file operations can thus be performed on a group of files with a single command.

- *Shell scripts*. A commonly used sequence of shell commands can be stored in a file. The name of the file can later be used to execute the stored sequence with a single command.
- *Shell variables*. The user can control the behavior of the shell, as well as other programs and utilities, by storing data in variables.
- *Programming language constructs*. The shell includes features that allow it to be used as a programming language. These features can be used to build shell scripts that perform complex operations.

Using the Bourne Shell

User interaction with the shell takes the form of a dialog. First, the shell asks the user for input, then the user types a command, and finally the shell causes the command to be carried out. When the command's task has been completed, the shell once again asks the user for input, the user types a command, and so on. When the shell is ready for command input, the shell displays a *prompt* on the terminal screen, usually a *dollar sign* (**$**). Figure 6.1 shows the sequence of steps in a user's dialog with the shell.

The shell itself does not carry out most of the commands that are typed to it. Instead, the shell examines each command and starts the appropriate XENIX utility program that carries out the requested action. The shell can easily determine which utility program to start because the name of the command and the name of the utility program are the same! The standard XENIX system comes with over two hundred utility programs. (One of these utilities is **sh**—the Bourne shell itself.)

User programs are started in the same way as the XENIX utilities. The user types the name of the program as a command, and the shell executes the program on the user's behalf.

Shell Commands

All commands typed to the shell have a similar format, shown in figure 6.2. A command line consists of a sequence of words, each sep-

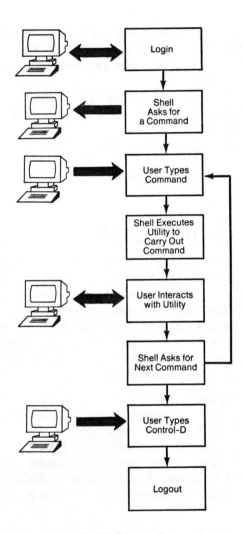

Fig. 6.1. Using the Bourne shell.

arated by one or more spaces. The first word is the *command* itself,
which is the name of the utility or user program to be executed, and
which tells the shell "what" to do. The remaining words are command options and arguments. An *option* controls "how" the com-

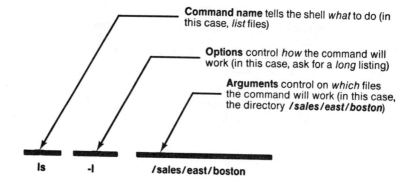

Command name tells the shell *what* to do (in this case, *list* files)

Options control *how* the command will work (in this case, ask for a *long* listing)

Arguments control on *which* files the command will work (in this case, the directory */sales/east/boston*)

ls   -l   /sales/east/boston

Fig. 6.2. Bourne shell command structure.

mand is to be performed. An *argument*, usually a file name, indicates on "which" files (or other items) the command will operate. In figure 6.2 the **ls** utility displays the file names in a directory. The **-l** option requests the long form of the command output. Finally, the **/sales/east/boston** argument tells which directory to look in for the file names and information.

Command Input and Output

Most XENIX utility programs perform one simple, well-defined function. They take some data as input, perform some processing on the data, and produce the results as output. When a user requests execution of a program by typing its name as a shell command, the shell runs the program and assigns to it three standard files:

- A *standard input* file, from which the program takes its input data
- A *standard output* file, which receives the output of the program
- A *standard error* file, which receives any error messages generated during processing

Figure 6.3 illustrates this structure.

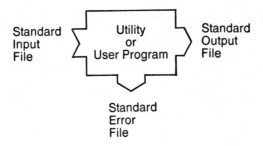

Fig. 6.3. Standard files.

Normally, the shell launches a program with all three of its standard files automatically assigned to the user's terminal. When the program requests input, it comes from the terminal keyboard. When the program produces output or error messages, they appear on the terminal display. Figure 6.4 shows the assignment of the standard input, output, and error files to the terminal.

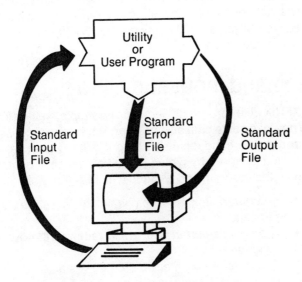

Fig. 6.4. Standard file assignments.

Input/Output Redirection

One of the most powerful features of the shell is its ability to reassign the standard input and output files of a command. This capability is known as input and output *redirection*. For example, suppose a program named **inquiry** takes a list of one or more customer numbers as its input and presents data from a customer master file as its output. Normally, the program will take its input from the terminal and display its output on the screen, as in the following example:

```
$ inquiry
12345

Customer #:    12345
Name:          Consolidated Industries
Address:       1234 Chestnut St.
City:          Maintown
State:         CA
Zip:           01234
Balance:       $22,126.78
   .
   .
   .
```

If the **inquiry** program is to be executed for a list of one hundred customers, typing the customer numbers, one by one, as input to the **inquiry** program, would be tedious and might introduce errors. Alternatively, the list of customer numbers can be placed in a file, using one of the XENIX text-editing utilities. The user can then *redirect* the standard input of the **inquiry** program to this file. If the file **numbers** contains the list of customer numbers, then the command

```
$ inquiry < numbers
   .
   .
   .
```

will generate the customer information for the list of customers. The *less than sign* (<) instructs the shell to launch the **inquiry** program, taking its standard input from the file **numbers** rather than the terminal keyboard.

Similarly, the output of a program can be redirected to a file other than the terminal display. The command

```
$ inquiry > /dev/lp
   .
   .
   .
```

causes the **inquiry** program to take its customer numbers from the terminal keyboard, but to display its output on the printer (named **/dev/lp**) instead of the terminal display. The *greater than sign* (>) instructs the shell to redirect the standard output of the **inquiry** program.

Both the standard input and output files of a program can be redirected at the same time, as in the following command:

```
$ inquiry < numbers > custinfo
$ ■
```

In this case, the **inquiry** program takes its input from the file named **numbers** and sends its output to the file named **custinfo**. Figure 6.5 graphically illustrates the effects of I/O redirection.

Output redirected to a file normally causes existing contents of the file to be overwritten. However, output can be added to the end of a file by using two adjacent greater than signs (>>) in place of the >. There are a number of other variations to the redirection facility of the shell, but their uses are beyond the scope of this book.

Recall that a major feature of the XENIX file system is file and device independence. Combined with the shell's input/output redirection capability, this feature becomes even more powerful. With file and device independence, any program written to process data from one type of file or device can be used with other files and devices *without changing the program.*

The user can choose the actual files or input/output devices to be used by a program just before the program is run. This selection op-

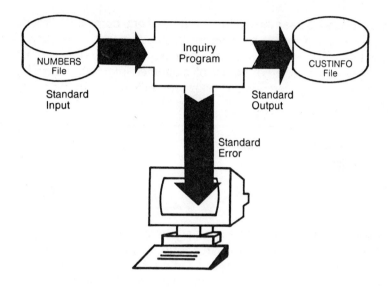

Fig. 6.5. I/O redirection with the shell.

portunity greatly increases the flexibility of the utilities and the user programs running on the XENIX system.

Pipes and Filters

Many useful XENIX utilities are designed to accept data from a single input file, process the data, and present the results on a single output file. Such a program is known as a *filter*. Like a mechanical filter, a XENIX filter selectively alters the data flowing through it. For example, the XENIX utility **dd** can be used as a filter to take an input file containing upper- and lowercase text and produce an output file with only uppercase text.

Generally, XENIX utilities are built to perform one simple function well. More complex tasks are accomplished by combining utilities in sequence, one after the other. This combining is possible through the XENIX pipe facility, one of the most celebrated features of the XENIX system.

A *pipe* is used to pass the standard output of one command directly to another command, to be used as its standard input. This capability is especially useful when two commands will be run sequentially. For example, a sorted list of customer information can be generated, using redirection, with the following sequence of commands:

```
$ sort numbers > tempfile
$ inquiry < tempfile
.
.
.
```

The **sort** command sorts the customer numbers for the inquiry and places the sorted list of numbers in a temporary file named **tempfile**. The **inquiry** command then takes its input from the temporary file and produces the customer information on the terminal display.

Alternatively, the same output can be generated without the use of a temporary file by using the pipe facility:

```
$ sort numbers | inquiry
.
.
.
```

The *vertical bar* (|) is the pipe character, instructing the shell to "pipe" the output of the **sort** command directly to the **inquiry** command as its input. Figure 6.6 illustrates the preceding example.

Note what has occurred here. Two simple programs, which had not been specifically written to work together, have been combined to form a "sorted-inquiry" function. This new function was created without writing any new programs. The ability to make new functions out of existing functions is a major benefit of the pipe facility.

With this facility, the shell allows any number of commands to be connected in a sequence, known as a *pipeline*. As in the previous example, the standard output of each command in the sequence (except the last) is "piped into" the standard input of the next command. Figure 6.7 illustrates the pipeline concept. All of the programs

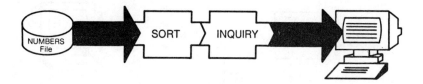

Fig. 6.6. The XENIX pipe feature.

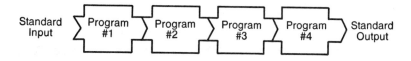

Fig. 6.7. A XENIX pipeline.

in a pipeline execute at the same time. XENIX automatically handles the data flow from one program to the next, producing the same effect as if one large program, rather than several smaller ones, had been executed.

The XENIX system includes many file-processing utilities that can be used as filters. Utilities are available to select lines from a file, sort the lines into order, reformat the lines, and so on. By combining these utilities into pipelines, most file-processing functions can be performed without writing new programs.

Pipe Fitting

Generally, the intermediate output files of a pipeline are of no use outside the pipeline. The kernel simply discards the files' contents after the pipeline has finished its work. The **tee** utility is used to preserve an intermediate output file from within a pipeline, for later processing. Figure 6.8 shows how **tee** operates. It copies each line from the standard input file to the standard output file, but **tee** also

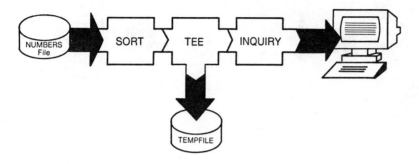

*Fig. 6.8. Pipe fitting with the **tee** utility.*

copies the line to one or more other files, identified by name. Thus, the pipeline

> **$ sort numbers | tee tempfile | inquiry**
> .
> .
> .

preserves the sorted list of customer numbers from the previous example in a file named **tempfile**.

Wild-Card Matching

Users of a XENIX system often need to perform a file-processing operation on an entire group of files. For example, a user may want to remove all the files in a certain directory. Or perhaps all the files that relate to forecasting have names beginning with the letters *fore* and must be copied to another directory for processing. The shell allows a user to perform these operations on a group of files, with a single command, through the shell's "wild card" matching facility.

The shell interprets two characters as *wild cards*. When these characters are used in a file name as part of a shell command line, they are interpreted in a special way. The *asterisk* (*) matches any sequence of zero or more characters in a file name. The *question mark*

(**?**) matches exactly one character. A few examples illustrate this concept clearly.

If the user wanted to delete all the files in the current directory, the following command would achieve this effect:

```
$ rm *
$ ■
```

Because the asterisk matches any number of characters in a file name, the asterisk matches all the file names in the directory (all of which contain from one to fourteen characters). Similarly, the command

```
$ rm fore*
$ ■
```

will remove all file names that begin with the four characters *fore*. Files named **forecast**, **forecast1**, **forecast10**, and **fore** will be removed, whereas files named **oldforecast** or **for** will not be removed.

For single-character matching, the question mark wild-card character is used. For example, the command

```
$ rm forecast?
$ ■
```

will remove the files named **forecast1** and **forecastx**, but not the file named **forecast** or **forecast10** because the question mark must match exactly one character.

The shell offers a more precise kind of wild-card matching that resembles the matching behavior of the question mark but restricts the characters that will be matched. A list of characters enclosed in *square brackets* (**[ ]**) will match any one of the designated characters. For example, the command

```
$ rm forecast[123]
$ ■
```

will remove files named **forecast1**, **forecast2**, and **forecast3**, but will not remove a file named **forecast5** or **forecast**. The same effect can also be achieved with a range of characters, instead of a list, as in the following:

```
$ rm forecast[1-3]
$ ■
```

Wild-card characters can be intermixed with regular characters in a file name, such as **for??ast[13]**. All the wild-card-matching features can be used any time that a file name appears in a shell command. Wild-card matching provides a convenient way to manipulate groups of files as a unit.

Background Processing

Normally, the dialog between the user and the shell, and between the user and the XENIX utilities, happens interactively. A user initiates only one activity at a time, and the shell waits until the activity is complete before prompting the user for the next command.

Some time-consuming tasks do not require interaction with the user. These include long-running report programs or programs that perform end-of-month update functions. Executing these tasks interactively would tie up a user terminal unnecessarily. To eliminate this problem, a user may request *background* execution (processing) of a time-consuming task. The shell will launch the program and then prompt the user immediately for the next command. In this way, the user may continue with other work while the task is being performed.

A user requests background execution of a program by placing an *ampersand* (**&**) at the end of a command line. For example, the following command will run the **inquiry** program *in the background*, sending its output to the printer:

```
$ inquiry < numbers > /dev/lp &
4567
$ ■
```

The shell displays an identifying number for the background task and then prompts for the next command. The user is immediately free to type another command and to execute additional programs while the background program continues to execute. By requesting background execution over and over again, a user can cause the XENIX system to work on several tasks at once. Figure 6.9 illustrates background processing.

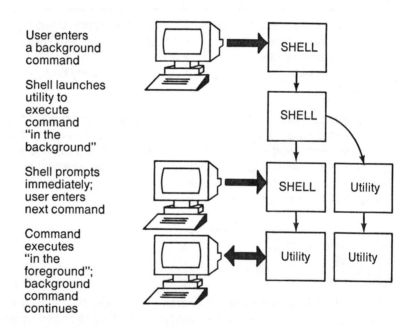

User enters
a background
command

Shell launches
utility to
execute
command
"in the
background"

Shell prompts
immediately;
user enters
next command

Command
executes
"in the
foreground";
background
command
continues

Fig. 6.9. Background processing.

Shell Scripts

Most XENIX system users find that they use the same sequences of shell commands over and over again. These command sequences can be stored in a file called a *shell script*. The entire sequence of commands in the script can then be executed simply by typing the name of the file as a command to the shell.

For example, suppose that sales results for each week of the month are stored in files named **week1, week2, week3,** and **week4.** The usual procedure at the end of each month is to combine the weekly results into a single file, named **results,** for the month. A monthly sales report is printed, and the weekly sales files are then removed. The following sequence of four shell commands accomplishes the end-of-month procedure for the Boston office:

```
$ cd /sales/east/boston      # move to the boston directory
$ cat week? > results        # concatenate four weekly files
$ report < results           # print monthly report
$ rm week?                   # remove the weekly files
$ ■
```

The same four commands can be typed each month, but this kind of repetitive typing can be avoided with shell scripts. Using one of the standard XENIX text editors, the user can prepare a four-line file containing the sequence of commands. If this file were named **end-month,** then the end-of-month procedure could be accomplished simply by giving the command

```
$ endmonth
$ ■
```

The shell will examine the file **endmonth** and execute the commands stored there, one after another, just as if they had been typed at the terminal keyboard. The shell prompts the user for the next command only after all the commands in the script have been executed. All the facilities of the shell, including wild-card matching and background processing, can be used within shell scripts.

Shell Variables

Simple shell scripts can be used as convenient typing aids because they replace an entire sequence of command lines with a single command typed by the user. However, this use of shell scripts is also inflexible because the sequence of commands will be executed exactly the same way each time the script is invoked. As a result, ten different shell scripts would be required to run the end-of-month procedure for each of ten sales offices.

Shell scripts can be made more flexible by using a feature of the shell called shell variables. A *shell variable* is a name that is used to store a string of characters. The *value of the variable is the character string. Like file names, variable names can be any sequence of characters, and the names are usually chosen to describe the kind of information the variables store. For example, a variable named* **OFFICE** might be used to store the name of a particular sales office. The value of the variable might be "boston" or "newyork."

A variable is assigned a value by typing the variable's name, followed by an *equal sign* (=), followed by the value. Typing

```
$ OFFICE=boston
$ ■
```

to the shell gives the value "boston" to the variable named **OFFICE**.

The value of a variable can later be retrieved for use in a shell command. A *dollar sign* ($) followed by a variable name instructs the shell to substitute the value of the variable in place of the variable name before executing the command. For example, the command

```
$ cd /sales/east/$OFFICE
$ ■
```

will make **/sales/east/boston** the current working directory. Before executing the **cd** command, the shell substitutes the value "boston" for the variable named **OFFICE**. The net effect of the command is the same as if the user had typed the following:

cd /sales/east/boston

Shell variables are especially useful in shell scripts, allowing the script behavior to vary, based on the value of one or more variables. The **endmonth** script in the example earlier can be made more flexible with shell variables. The following modified script can be used to perform the end-of-month procedure for *any* of the sales offices, depending on the value of the variable **OFFICE**:

```
cd /sales/east/$OFFICE     # move to the $OFFICE directory
cat week? > results        # concatenate four weekly files
report < results           # print monthly report
rm week?                   # remove the weekly files
```

This procedure can be performed for the New York sales office, for example, with these commands:

```
$ OFFICE=newyork
$ export OFFICE
$ endmonth
$ ■
```

The **export** command simply makes the value of the variable **OF-FICE** available to the **endmonth** script. With the use of shell variables, the script has been made more general, and the need for a different script for each office has been eliminated.

Special Shell Variables

By convention, the XENIX system stores in shell variables several important pieces of information, which vary from user to user. For example, the shell finds it convenient to know the name of a user's home directory. Other programs may need to know the kind of terminal being used. Table 6.1 lists some of the special variables used by the shell and other XENIX utilities.

The special shell variable **PATH** controls which program or utility is executed when a user types a command to the shell. The **PATH** variable holds a particular sequence of directory names. When the user types a command, the shell searches these directories, in the order named in the **PATH** variable, to find the utility or user program with the same name as the command name and to execute it. The sequence of directory names is known as a *search path*.

PATH	A list of directories to be searched by the shell to find programs whose names are typed as commands
TERM	The kind of terminal being used
HOME	The name of the user's home directory
MAIL	The name of the user's mailbox for the XENIX mail facility
PS1	The string that is used by the shell to prompt for the next command (usually "$ ")
SHELL	The name of the user's shell
TZ	The time zone

Table 6.1. Special Shell Variables

A typical search path might include the following three directory names:

PATH=/bin:/usr/bin:/sales/programs

The colons in the search path separate the directory names in the list. Recall that most standard shell commands are simply the names of utility programs. By convention, the utilities are stored in the directories named **/bin** and **/usr/bin**. These directories will be included by most XENIX users in their search paths, to instruct the shell to look there automatically for XENIX commands.

With search paths, the names of user programs stored in other directories can also be typed to the shell as commands. For example, if the **endmonth** script were stored in the directory **/sales/programs,** then the inclusion of this directory in the search path allows the user to type **endmonth** as a shell command. The shell will successfully find the script and execute it. Because each user may have a different search path, each user can create a personalized set of commands.

The Shell as a Programming Language

In addition to its role as an interactive command interpreter, the shell can be used as a powerful programming language. Two of its programming language features have already been described—shell scripts and shell variables. Many such programming language features are available, allowing users to create sophisticated scripts that accomplish complex tasks. These features include the following:

- *Scripts.* A sequence of commands can be stored in a file for later execution.
- *Variables. Values stored in named variables can be used within shell scripts.*
- *Arguments.* Data can be passed to variables within a shell script by typing the values as arguments on the command line.
- *Conditional execution.* The sequence of executed commands can be varied, based on some external condition. (**if...then...else** command)
- *Case selection.* One of several alternative command sequences can be selected for execution, based on some external condition. (**case** command)
- *Repetition.* A sequence of commands can be executed repeatedly for a list of values, each time assigning the next value to a shell variable. (**for** command)
- *Conditional repetition.* A sequence of commands can be executed repeatedly until some external condition occurs. (**while** command)
- *Command substitution.* The standard output of a command in a script may be redirected into the script itself, becoming part of another command.
- *Comments.* Descriptive text can be included in a shell script to help explain its operation.

An Example of a Shell Script

The shell's programming language constructs are normally used by sophisticated XENIX users with some programming background. Shell scripts are often used in place of actual programs written in languages like BASIC, C, or Pascal. In fact, several XENIX system utilities are actually sophisticated shell scripts. Figure 6.10 shows a relatively simple shell script that uses programming constructs.

```
# This script performs the end-of-month procedure for each
# sales office in the eastern region.
#
for OFFICE in newyork boston phila  # For each office ...
    do
    cd /sales/east/$OFFICE            # move to the correct
                                      # directory ...
    cat week? > results              # perform the
    report < results                 # end-of-month
    rm week?                         # procedure ...
    echo Finished with $OFFICE       # ... and print a
                                     # message.
    done
echo All sales reports complete      # Indicate when
                                     # complete.
```

Fig. 6.10. A shell script with programming constructs.

The **for** command in the script causes the sequence of commands between the **do** and **done** commands to be executed once for each office. When the sequence of commands is executed, the value of the shell variable **OFFICE** will be "newyork," then "boston," and then "phila." The command sequence executed for each office is unchanged from the previous end-of-month procedure. The **echo** commands display informational messages on the terminal screen as the script executes. All text following the *pound sign* (#) on each line of the script is a comment, which is ignored by the shell.

Utilities for Building Shell Scripts

Several shell utilities are especially useful for constructing shell scripts. For example, it is often useful to have a script display messages on the terminal screen as the script executes. Or a script may need to test the value of a shell variable or check to see whether a

echo	Displays a prompt or message on the standard output file
read	Reads values from the standard input file into shell variables
line	Reads one line of text from the standard input file and copies the line to the standard output file
test	Tests for various conditions, such as the existence of a file; useful for controlling conditional script execution
expr	Evaluates an expression and outputs its value
true	Returns a *true* value; useful for condition testing
false	Returns a *false* value; useful for condition testing
wait	Waits for the completion of background processing; is used to ensure that critical processing is complete before proceeding in a script
sleep	Causes command execution to stop for a specified number of seconds

Table 6.2. Useful Utilities for Building Shell Scripts

required file is present before trying to use it. Table 6.2 lists the utilities that perform these and other functions which are particularly useful for script building.

The C Shell

The C shell (**csh**), an alternative command interpreter for the XENIX system, was originally offered as part of the Berkeley version of UNIX. This shell is very similar to the Bourne shell; in fact, most of the commands are exactly the same in both shells. But the C shell also includes several built-in "convenience" features that make it a very efficient tool for expert XENIX users.

One of the C shell's most powerful capabilities is its *history list* feature. The C shell automatically saves the commands that a user types, to form a *command history*. The user can display this history and also reuse commands or parts of commands through a shorthand notation. The *exclamation point* character (!), when typed to the C shell, invokes the history feature. The characters immediately following the exclamation point control which part of the command history will be reused.

For example, typing

```
% !c
% ■
```

causes the C shell to reexecute the most recent command that began with the letter *c*. Note that the percent sign (%) is the C shell prompt. Similarly, the command

```
% !!
% ■
```

causes the C shell to repeat the last command. The user can also reuse just the arguments of a previous command. In the example

```
% ls text1 text2
text1
text2
% cat !*
   .
   .
   .
```

the user first confirms with the **ls** command that two files are in the current directory, then displays their contents with the **cat** command. The **!*** characters instruct the C shell to reuse the file list, thus saving keystrokes.

The shorthand capabilities of the history mechanism are much more sophisticated than these examples demonstrate. Using the C shell, a user can isolate individual words of a previous command for reuse and even edit a previous command before reusing it. Although the history mechanism may appear confusing to the novice, in the hands of an experienced user, the mechanism can save considerable typing. This is especially true in software development applications, where the same sequence of commands is often repeated over and over.

Another useful C shell feature is its **alias** facility. With this feature, the user can give a command or phrase an *alias*—a single word that will be used as an abbreviation. For example, a PC DOS user accustomed to using the **dir** command to list file names might establish the following alias:

```
% alias dir ls -l
%
```

Once the alias has been established, the C shell automatically substitutes the full command or phrase every time the alias appears in a command typed to it. The **unalias** command deletes aliases that are no longer needed.

The C shell provides a protection against accidentally overwriting existing files. When the shell variable **noclobber** is set on, the C shell will prevent the standard output from being redirected to an already existing file. The C shell also supports shell scripts, but the commands that control the flow of script execution are somewhat different from those of the Bourne shell. The C shell flow control commands resemble the corresponding constructs in the C programming language, hence, the name C shell.

The Visual Shell

The visual shell (**vsh**), a menu-driven user interface to the XENIX system, simplifies its operation for end-users. Both the Bourne shell and the C shell require that a user know the names of the XENIX commands in advance—the shells simply display a prompt, and the user must type a valid command. In contrast, the visual shell presents the user with a menu of choices. The user always knows what options are available at any time and simply chooses one of them.

The user interface of the visual shell resembles that of the PC applications packages available from Microsoft, such as Multiplan. The visual shell uses a full-screen display, as shown in figure 6.11.

To use the visual shell, the user chooses a command from the menu line. The space bar moves the cursor from choice to choice, and the

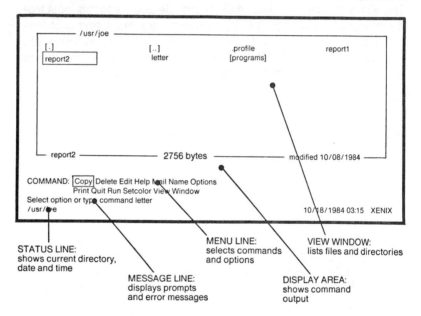

Fig. 6.11. The visual shell.

return key makes the selection. As a shortcut, typing the first letter of a command automatically selects a menu choice. Once a command has been selected, more menus may be displayed, offering a choice of command options.

For commands that use files, the view window provides an easy way to select specific files for processing. A list of the currently available files is always displayed in the view window, and the cursor keys on the keyboard move within the list for selection.

The view window can also be used for conveniently browsing the contents of files and directories. Pressing the equal sign (=) key causes the visual shell to "zoom in" on the contents of the selected file or directory. Zooming in on a directory displays a list of the files contained in the directory; zooming in on a file displays its contents. Pressing the minus sign (-) key zooms back out to the previous viewing level.

The visual shell's command menus provide access to the most frequently used XENIX commands for file management, text processing, and electronic mail. More advanced XENIX commands are available through the **RUN** menu selection, which allows the user to type the name of any XENIX command or shell script.

7

Multiuser Operation

XENIX is a multiuser operating system by design. Multiuser capabilities were incorporated into the UNIX system very soon after its creation to support within Bell Labs programming groups that needed a shared system for software development. XENIX has inherited these multiuser capabilities and has added new features to simplify multiuser processing and system administration. Typical XENIX-based microcomputer systems are used by as few as one or as many as a dozen simultaneous users, and XENIX supports diverse applications, such as the following:

- *Software development.* A group of programmers can use XENIX software development tools to develop their own programs, while sharing common modules, such as file definitions and subroutines.
- *Text processing.* A group of writers can use XENIX text-processing tools to prepare individual sections of a single document, such as an administrative manual or a technical manuscript.

- *Applications processing.* In a small business, clerical personnel can use a system for accounting, inventory control, and order-processing tasks and can share common data among the departments.

A single XENIX system can also intermix these different types of use, making XENIX a powerful, general-purpose solution to many different application problems. This chapter describes the XENIX features and commands that support multiuser operation.

Multiuser Features and Benefits

The major XENIX system features that support multiuser operation are the following:

- *Multiprocessing.* XENIX supports multiple users through concurrent execution of multiple programs. Individual users may also execute multiple programs concurrently.
- *System security.* A user password scheme controls access to the XENIX system.
- *File security.* Access to XENIX files is controlled on a user-by-user basis; three different forms of file access can be selectively allowed or disallowed.
- *Spooling.* XENIX system utilities manage shared access to printers by multiple users.
- *Accounting.* XENIX monitors usage of system resources and maintains accounting records.
- *System administration.* XENIX provides utilities for system maintenance and administration functions, such as backup and error recovery.

The Concept of a Process

The fundamental unit of multiuser XENIX operation is the *process.* Simply stated, a process is a program in a state of execution. When a user runs a program on the XENIX system, the running program is called a process. We speak of processes "doing things," as in "this process is printing checks on the printer," or "this process will open three files and merge their contents." A process is a program doing useful work on a XENIX system.

XENIX supports multiple users by allowing multiple processes to execute concurrently. A small desktop XENIX system, such as the IBM PC AT, may have as many as ten processes in execution at one time. A larger XENIX system, supporting a dozen users, may have several dozen processes in concurrent execution. XENIX uses processes liberally. Almost nothing gets done in a XENIX system without creating a process to perform the task.

Of course, XENIX systems have only one central processor; therefore, the system can actually be working on only one process at a time. The system creates the illusion of serving many users simultaneously by switching the CPU—very rapidly—from one process to the next. Because a typical XENIX system executes many thousands of instructions each second, the CPU can make quite a bit of progress on each user's work, even during a short period of time.

User Names

A typical XENIX system will have many different users. Each authorized user of the system is identified by a unique *user name*, containing up to eight characters. First names, last names, and job titles are often used as user names. XENIX uses the user name in several different ways. Accounting reports that show system usage are frequently sorted by user name. Utilities that list the people currently working on the system will display a list of user names. One of the most important functions of user names is to aid in implementing system and file security.

Because XENIX finds it easier to deal with numbers than with names, each user name corresponds to a unique user number known as a *user-id*, which is used internally within XENIX. User-id's sometimes appear in place of user names in XENIX reports and command output. The system administrator maintains the list of authorized user names, which is stored, along with other important information about each user, in the file **/etc/passwd**.

User Groups

Each XENIX system user may be a member of one or more *user groups* known to the system. User groups are usually comprised of users with related job functions or with similar needs for access to data. For example, in a small company, order-processing clerks may comprise one group; accounting clerks, another group; and the accounting supervisors who generate monthly reports, yet another group. Normally, the system administrator maintains the list of groups and group memberships, which is kept in the file **/etc/ group**. User groups form a part of the XENIX file security scheme.

A user group is identified by a name, which contains up to eight characters. Again, the system finds it more convenient to deal internally with the corresponding *group-id* number. A typical user group arrangement is illustrated in figure 7.1. As the figure shows, a user may be a member of more than one group. Membership, however, can be *active* in only one group at any one time. A XENIX utility is used to change the active group membership from one group to another.

Marketing Group   Accounting Group

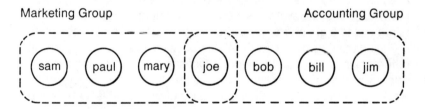

Fig. 7.1. User names and user groups.

XENIX Security

One of the key concerns on any multiuser computer system is the security of both the system and the data stored in it. Therefore, good security and protection features are much more important in the XENIX system than in personal computer operating systems.

Security in a personal computer is generally easy to maintain. Simply locking away the computer and the floppy disks that contain private data is usually adequate. In contrast, the data on a typical XENIX system is stored on a nonremovable disk. The system may have many attached terminals scattered throughout a building. Dial-in lines may also permit access from terminals in other locations. Thus, physical security of a XENIX system is difficult to maintain. In addition, the data stored on a typical XENIX system belongs to many individual users who expect their data to be kept private, even from other authorized users of the system.

XENIX concentrates its security features at the following two levels:

- *System level security.* XENIX restricts access to the system to only authorized users through a login/logout scheme.
- *File level security.* XENIX provides privacy for stored data through a file access permission scheme.

Logging In

XENIX implements system level security through its *login* proce-dure. Before granting access to the system, XENIX requests a user name from the prospective user, then checks the reply against the list of authorized user names. XENIX grants access to the system only if the name is found in the list.

In addition, XENIX provides an extra measure of security by allowing each user to have a password associated with the user's name. Without passwords, security of a XENIX system would be very low because the names of authorized users may be well known to others seeking access. If a user name is password-protected, the login procedure will demand both the user name and the corresponding password from the prospective user. To minimize the risk of a pass-word being accidentally revealed, XENIX turns off the display of typed characters on the terminal screen while the user types the password. A typical login sequence is included in figure 7.2.

XENIX stores encrypted versions of user passwords, along with the corresponding user names, in the **/etc/passwd** file. When the user types a password during the login sequence, the characters typed are encrypted, and the result is compared against the stored en-crypted password for the user. Thus, security derives primarily from the complex encryption method used and from the user's ability to change passwords frequently by using a XENIX utility program.

```
login: joe
Password:

/**********************************/
    Welcome to the Sales Dept System
/**********************************/
you have mail

$ pwd
/sales/east/boston
$ ls
forecast
orders
personnel
results
$ cat forecast
Smith    $10,654        12/83    Acme Fish Market
Smith    $ 2,450        11/83    John's Hardware
Harris   $13,295        10/83    Wayland Distributing
Harris   $ 4,270        11/83    Wayland Distributing
Jones    $ 2,235        10/83    Central Transportation
$
login:
```

Fig. 7.2. A short XENIX session.

Logging Out

Once a user has logged in to the system, the user's work session continues until the user instructs the shell to terminate the session. A user *logs out* by typing the *end-of-file* character (**Control-D**) to the shell, instead of typing a command. The system displays the **login:** prompt on the terminal display and awaits login by the next user.

File Access Permissions

XENIX implements a second level of security to protect a user's files against unauthorized access by other users of the system. Each file and directory in a XENIX system has exactly one user who is the *owner* of the file. The owner is typically the user who originally created the file. Each file also has a *group owner*, which is one of the user groups on the system.

In addition to information about the file's ownership, a set of *file access permissions* is maintained for each file and directory. These permissions determine which users may access the file and what kinds of file access will be permitted.

The following three types of file access can be granted or denied:

- *Read access* allows examination of a file's contents. The file may be displayed on a terminal, copied, compiled, etc., if a user has read access to it.
- *Write access* allows both modifying a file's contents and adding information to the file. The file may be altered or deleted if a user has write access to it.
- *Execute access* allows execution of a file as a program.

Each of these three types of file access may be selectively granted or denied to the following three different classes of users:

- The *owner* of the file
- Users in the *group owner* of the file
- *Other users* of the system

Figure 7.3 illustrates the nine file access permissions (three types of access for each of three classes of users) that are available for each file. Permissions offer a fair amount of flexibility in establishing file security. For example, in a small business, the company controller might be granted read and write access to the personnel file, whereas the accounting clerks, as a group, have only read access to process payrolls. The rest of the company is denied any access at all. In contrast, the budget report files are open to all users for read access but can be updated only by clerks in the accounting group. The report programs that generate the budget reports are open to the accounting group for execute access, but no one has write access to these same programs, to prevent accidental destruction.

File access permissions apply also to directories and special files. Read access to a directory allows a user to list the files in the directory. Write access allows a user to add new files to the directory. Finally, execute access to a directory allows a user to make that directory the user's own working directory.

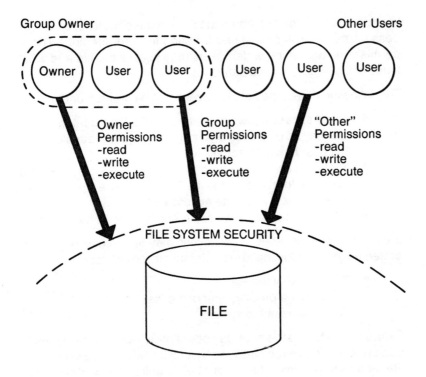

Fig. 7.3. File system security.

The Super-User

Certain administrative functions on a XENIX system require access to files and commands that are normally denied to all users. Adding a new name to the list of authorized user names is an example of one of these functions. On a multiuser XENIX system, these functions are usually performed by a system administrator, a "special" user charged with maintenance and general operation of the computer system. XENIX provides an exception to its file security scheme for this single user of the system, called the *super-user*.

By convention, the super-user is given the user name **root**. As the name implies, the super-user owns the root directory. The super-user also owns the directories and files that contain the XENIX operating system kernel, utilities, devices, etc. With this ownership, the super-user can authorize new users on the system and perform similar administrative functions.

All XENIX permission and protection mechanisms are bypassed for the super-user. The user name **root** is therefore always password-protected on a production XENIX system, and the password is supplied only on a "need to know" basis. Protection of the super-user password is the most critical link in preserving a XENIX system's security and integrity.

Multiprocessing Utilities

Several XENIX utilities are useful for monitoring and controlling the multiuser operation of the XENIX system. These include utilities for monitoring system activity and managing file security. Table 7.1 lists the most frequently used multiprocessing utilities.

Displaying Current Users

The **who** (**who** is on the system) utility displays the names of users currently logged on to a XENIX system, as in this example:

```
$ who
paul      tty7                11:40
jim       tty10       8:30
joe       tty3        2:00
mary      tty12       9:20
sam       tty4        3:08
$ ■
```

A special option to the **who** utility identifies the user who requested the command, as in the following example:

```
$ who am i
jim       tty10       8:30
$ ■
```

who	Displays the names of users currently logged in
ps	Displays process status information
whodo	Displays information about what each user is doing
finger	Displays detailed information about each user currently logged in
kill	Terminates a process
passwd	Changes a user's password
chown	Changes ownership of a file
chgrp	Changes the group owner of a file
chmod	Changes access permissions of a file
newgrp	Changes a user's active membership to a new group
su	Temporarily changes a user's user-Id
id	Displays a user's user- and group-ids and names
date	Displays the current date and time
at	Runs a command at a specified time
logname	Displays the user's login name

Table 7.1. Multiprocessing Utilities

Displaying Process Status

Another utility, **ps** (**p**rocess **s**tatus), displays information about the individual processes that are executing on the system:

```
$ ps
      PID  TTY  TIME   COMMAND
  rl64  10   0:24   sh
     1323 10   0:36   report
     1330 10   0:02   ps
$ ■
```

Each active process is identified by a unique number, called its *process-id* (PID). The **ps** utility displays the process-id, the terminal that controls the process, the cumulative execution time for the process, and the name of the command being executed. Options to the **ps** command control whether the utility displays information for only processes owned by the user, for all processes active on the system, and so on. Other options provide more detailed information, such as the state of the process (running, terminated, waiting, etc.) and the user-id of the user who owns the process.

Terminating Processes

Generally, processes are allowed to run to completion. The user can also forcefully terminate a process with the **kill** command:

```
$ kill 4637
$ ■
```

The **kill** command requires the process-id of the process to be terminated. Various options allow the user to send different *signals* to an executing process instead of killing the process directly. The process can detect these signals and will usually respond with an orderly shutdown of its operations before terminating.

Changing Passwords

The **passwd** (change **password**) utility allows a user to change the password associated with the user's name. The utility first prompts for the old password, then requests a new password—twice, to prevent typing errors. The new password is encrypted and saved, and it must be subsequently supplied by the user when logging into the system. The **passwd** utility is also used to establish a password for a new user.

Changing File Ownership

Two utilities are used to change the ownership of a file. The **chown** (**ch**ange **own**er) utility reassigns ownership of a file from one user to another. The **chgrp** (**ch**ange **gr**oup owner) performs the same function for the group that owns the file. For example, the command sequence

```
$ chown joe report1
$ chgrp finance report1
$ ■
```

will make the user named **joe** the owner of the **report1** file and will make the group named **finance** the group owner of the file.

Changing File Access Permissions

The **chmod** (**ch**ange **mod**e) utility changes the file access permissions for a file. Each one of the nine permissions (read, write, and execute for the owner, group owner, and others) can be individually granted or denied with this utility. The simple command

```
$ chmod +r report1
$ •
```

will grant read access (**+r**) to all three classes of users. The more complex example

```
$ chmod go-w report1
$ •
```

will deny write access (**-w**) to users in the group owning the file (**g**), as well as to all other users (**o**). Figure 7.4 shows how permissions are represented by the **ls** command and illustrates an alternative method of specifying file access permissions with the **chmod** utility.

Permissions in an LS command:

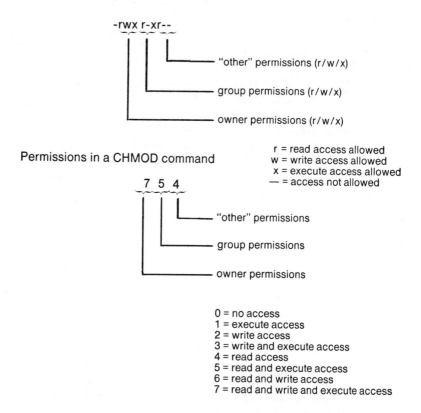

Fig. 7.4. Representing file access permissions.

Changing Groups

The **newgrp** (**new** user **gro**up) utility changes the user's active group membership from one user group to another. Typed by the user named **joe**, the command

```
$ newgrp acctng
$ ▪
```

will change the user's active group membership to the group named **acctng**. The utility verifies the user's membership in the new group before making it the active group.

Changing User-Id's

For convenience, XENIX provides a utility that allows a user to become another user, without first logging off the system and then logging back in. For example, a user may need temporary access to another user's files and may wish to assume that user's name for a short time. The **su** (become **s**uper **u**ser or another user) utility is used to change the user name (and the corresponding user-id) of a currently logged-in user. For example, if the user named **joe** types the command

```
$ su sam
Password:
$ ▮
```

Joe will temporarily assume the user name **sam** (and its corresponding user-id), and Joe will have access to Sam's files as if Joe had logged in as **sam**. If the new user name has an associated password, the **su** utility requests and validates it. The temporary identity lasts until the user types the end-of-file character to the shell, causing the user to revert back to the user's original user name. The **su** utility is also used to switch to super-user status by omitting the user name on the command line.

Spooling

In a multiuser environment, access to the system printer(s) must be carefully managed and controlled. Without this control, several users may attempt to send output to a printer at the same time, resulting in intermixed output on the printed pages. *Spooling* is a technique that allows each user to send output to the printer at will while the system manages the orderly printing of the output.

XENIX includes a spooling utility, called **lpr** (**l**ine **pr**inter spooler), that organizes multiuser access to the system printer. The utility operates by maintaining a list of disk files to be printed. A background process then prints the files, one at a time, on the system printer. Figure 7.5 illustrates spooling operation.

lpr has options that allow a user to delete automatically a file after printing or to be notified through the XENIX mail facility when printing is complete. Generally, **lpr** appears as the last program in a pipeline, where final output is to be printed. This program can also be used as a command, naming one or more files to be printed, as in

```
$ lpr report1 report2
$ ■
```

System Administration

In a multiuser computer system, several system administration functions must be performed on a periodic basis to ensure smooth and continued system operation. The system administration utilities provided in the UNIX system have been extended and modified in XENIX to simplify system administration. These utilities support the entire range of functions, including system configuration, user administration, multiuser accounting, and backup and recovery.

System Configuration

One of the system administrator's primary functions is configuring the XENIX system to match the particular hardware components of a computer system. For example, the **mkfs** (**make file system**) utility is used to set up a XENIX file system on a hard disk or a floppy disk. The **mount** (**mount** a file system) and **umount** (**unmount** a file system) utilities establish and remove access to these file systems. Other utilities perform similar functions for devices and terminals and also assist in orderly system shutdown. Table 7.2 lists the XENIX system configuration utilities.

User Administration

XENIX provides several utilities that simplify the task of keeping track of authorized users of a XENIX system. For example, the

mkuser (**make user**) and **rmuser** (remove **user**) utilities provide a convenient way to manage user access to the system. These utilities simplify the process of adding and removing authorized users by automatically updating the **/etc/passwd** and **/etc/group** files, creating login directories, etc. Other utilities check the integrity of the system files used for user administration.

Table 7.3 lists XENIX user administration utilities.

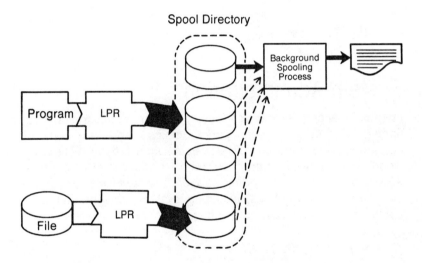

Fig. 7.5. Spooling operation.

Multiuser Accounting

The XENIX system optionally records system activity by maintaining a set of system log files. A set of accounting utilities prints reports based on the data in these files. The reports may be used to determine patterns of system use or to identify the need for additional memory, disk storage, terminals, etc. If a system is shared among different departments, the accounting reports can also be used as the basis of a billing scheme that fairly allocates the cost of system operation among the users.

mkfs	Constructs a file system on a hard disk or a floppy disk
mount	Attaches a file system to the root file system
umount	Detaches a file system from the root file system
format	Formats a floppy disk
mknod	Creates a directory entry for a "special" file
shutdown	Performs an orderly system shutdown after a specified delay
haltsys	Immediately shuts down the system
enable	Allows user logins from a particular terminal
disable	Disallows user logins from a particular terminal
fdisk	Creates and maintains disk partitions, thus allowing XENIX to coexist with other operating systems, such as MS-DOS
bdblkutil	Maintains the table of bad disk blocks

Table 7.2. System Configuration Utilities

The system maintains two separate log files to support accounting:

- On a *per-process* basis. The system records the name of the program executed, elapsed and CPU-times, main memory usage, and amount of I/O activity. The file also identifies the user-id, the group-id of the process, and the terminal from which the process was started.
- On a *per-login* basis. The system records the user's name, user-id, the CPU-time used, the terminal connect time, the number of processes executed, and disk usage information.

mkuser	Adds a new user to the list of authorized users of the system
rmuser	Removes a user from the list of authorized users
pwcheck	Checks the integrity of the **/etc/passwd** file
grpcheck	Checks the integrity of the **/etc/group** file
pwadmin	Performs password-aging administration

Table 7.3. User Administration Utilities

Backup and Recovery

System backup is an important administrative task on a busy multiuser XENIX system. Periodically copying active files from disk to a floppy disk or other backup medium protects users against accidental destruction or modification of important files. If an accident does occur, the backup copy of the file can be recovered. Standard XENIX utilities perform file backup and recovery functions. Two utilities used for this purpose are **cpio** (**c**opy **i**n/**o**ut) and **tar** (**t**ape **ar**chive).

Another group of XENIX utilities provides an incremental backup and recovery facility. With the **dump** utility, the system administrator can selectively back up only those files that have been modified since the last backup operation. The **dump** utility supports backups performed at different levels (for example, daily, weekly, or monthly). This utility allows the more frequently performed backups to be done quickly because they must record only the changes from the less frequent backups. The **restor** (**restor**e from backup) utility allows recovery of individual files or entire file systems.

Another administrative utility is used to verify file system integrity and to repair file systems that have been damaged by system failures. The **fsck** (**f**ile **s**ystem **c**heck) utility checks the directories and file relationships as they appear on the disk and also reports inconsistencies and errors. If the file system does contain errors, **fsck** allows the system administrator to recover as much of the file system as possible. The **fsck** utility is a privileged one that is available only to the super-user.

The XENIX disk buffering scheme presents another opportunity for a loss of data integrity because data held in the disk buffers may be lost during a system error, such as a power failure. The **sync** (**sync**hronize disk buffers) utility forces the contents of the disk buffers to be written to the disk immediately and not at the convenience of the system. Many installations arrange to have **sync** execute automatically every minute or so, assuring that inconsistencies between the disk and the file buffer are, at most, a minute old. The **sync** utility can be executed by any user.

Table 7.4 summarizes the administrative utilities for system backup and recovery.

cpio	Copies files to and from a backup medium and lists the contents of a backup tape or floppy disk
tar	An older but still popular file-backup utility, which performs the same functions as **cpio**
dump	Produces an incremental dump on a backup medium, such as a floppy disk
dumpdir	Lists the files produced by **dump** on a backup medium
restor	Restores files from an incremental dump
sddate	Sets and displays the date used for incremental dumps
sysadmin	Automatically performs file system backups and restores
fsck	Checks the integrity of file systems and performs repairs
sync	Forces the contents of the disk buffers to be copied to disk

Table 7.4. System Backup and Recovery Utilities

8

Turnkey Processing with XENIX

The XENIX system offers applications designers an excellent set of facilities for building turnkey applications systems. A turnkey system presents a user with an environment of familiar menus, forms, and application-oriented choices that make an application extremely easy to use. The user simply "turns the key" to start the system and is prompted and guided through a set of choices specific to the application. Once a turnkey application has been developed, XENIX can become an "invisible foundation" on top of which the application executes. The application user does not have to understand the XENIX system below, or even be aware of it.

This chapter describes the process management facilities of the XENIX system that make it well suited for turnkey applications processing. The chapter also describes some of the XENIX implementation techniques that make XENIX a particularly good foundation for building turnkey systems. Some of this latter information will be of interest only to applications designers. Nontechnical readers should feel free to skip these sections without fear of missing important information.

Turnkey Processing Facilities

XENIX facilities that support turnkey applications processing include the following:

- *System calls.* A set of over sixty system calls supports a variety of services and makes XENIX-based applications highly portable.
- *Process management.* The XENIX multiprocessing structure provides a tool for organizing applications.
- *File sharing and locking.* XENIX provides a mechanism for applications programs to synchronize concurrent update to a shared file.
- *Device sharing.* A process can obtain temporary exclusive access to a device such as a floppy disk.
- *Process scheduling.* XENIX uses scheduling algorithms that favor interactive, terminal-oriented tasks, keeping user response times low.
- *Memory management.* XENIX efficiently allocates main memory among concurrently executing tasks. The technique of swapping permits effective interactive operation, even when memory is not large enough to hold all concurrently executing processes.
- *Pipes and interprocess communication.* The ability to pass data between processes allows sophisticated applications architectures to be built with the XENIX system.
- *Shared memory and semaphores.* Processes can also communicate by passing data through a shared portion of main memory.
- *Tailorable start-up procedures.* The XENIX start-up procedures can be customized to perform application-specific functions automatically.
- *Alternative user interfaces.* The XENIX system shells can be replaced with a user-developed program that provides an applications-oriented user interface to the XENIX system.
- *Terminal-independent applications.* Applications programs can use XENIX system facilities to insulate themselves from the particular characteristics of different brands of terminals that may be used on a XENIX system.

- *Shell scripts.* The shell forms an effective programming language for binding together applications programs into a total applications system. Shell scripts were discussed in Chapter 6.

XENIX System Calls

The XENIX system call is the structure used by an application program to request services from the XENIX system kernel. System calls perform a variety of functions for applications programs. The calls are used, for example, to perform input and output, to create and remove files, to control processes, and to communicate between them. The set of approximately sixty system calls forms the interface between an application program and the XENIX system kernel.

Every XENIX system has exactly the same set of system calls, which perform exactly the same set of functions. The internals of the XENIX kernel may be different between versions of XENIX running on the Motorola 68000 and the PC AT's Intel 80286, but both systems will offer exactly the same set of system calls. The system call interface is a standard, which is unchanged from XENIX system to XENIX system.

This standardization makes applications software written for XENIX highly portable. An application program, such as a word processor, built on the system call interface, will execute on any XENIX system. No changes to the program's source code are required to move the program from one system to another. Applications developers can write their programs without having to worry about adapting them to run on different XENIX systems.

A detailed discussion of the system calls is beyond the scope of this text. They are of concern mainly to programmers, and even then, the system calls are usually used indirectly through the C language library routines. Appendix A lists the XENIX system calls, with a short description of each.

Process Management

The XENIX system's process management facilities allow applications programs to be efficiently structured. Foreground processes can interact with users, while background processes execute concurrently to handle noninteractive tasks. A process may start other processes to accomplish subtasks within an application. Interprocess communications facilities are also available to coordinate the work of the processes that comprise an application.

Recall that a process is a program in a state of execution. A process begins its life at the beginning of a program and lives as long as the program's instructions continue to specify new operations. When the program finally reaches a **halt**, **stop**, or **return** instruction (depending on the processor), the program terminates, and the process dies. Several XENIX system calls are available that alter the normal life cycle of a process.

The **exec** System Call

A single process may execute several different programs during its life by making use of the **exec** system call. Figure 8.1 shows what happens when a process makes this call. The kernel "transforms" the process into an execution of a new program. The kernel loads the new program into memory and resumes execution of the process at its beginning. The name of the new program is specified in the **exec** system call.

The new program begins execution with a considerable amount of history from its predecessor. Files opened by the previous program remain open for the new program. The process also retains its user-id and group-id.

Figure 8.2 shows a simple example of how a sequence of report programs may be executed, using the **exec** call. The first program prints the first report before the program "execs" the second report program. The second program adds its report to the output file and execs the third report program, which finally closes the files and ends the process. The **exec** system call can be used much like the "program chaining" capability available in many other operating systems.

Fig. 8.1. The **exec** *system call.*

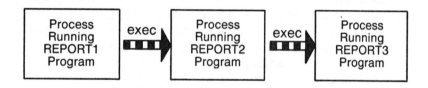

Fig. 8.2. An **exec** *example.*

The *fork* System Call

New processes are created in only one way: a currently active process requests creation of a new process through the **fork** system call. The new process that results is called the *child* process, and the original process is called the *parent* process. After the **fork**, both the parent and child processes are in execution. These processes are executing identical copies of the same program, with the same open files. Forking resembles the biological division of a cell into two identical cells.

Typically, the parent and child processes will not continue to execute the same program for very long. Immediately after the **fork** has been made, the child process will usually exec a new program. The result of the **fork/exec** combination is to create a new process that executes a new program. Both the parent and child processes are free to fork other processes, creating a hierarchy of processes with parent/child relationships.

The process hierarchy provides a natural way to structure menu-driven applications. Figure 8.3 shows a typical example, in which a **menu** program offers a choice of three data entry screens. When the user makes a selection, the **menu** program forks a child process, which execs the chosen program, and the data entry program runs to completion. Meanwhile, the **menu** program waits for completion of its child process, with a **wait** system call. Further execution of the **menu** program will resume when the data entry process dies. Figure 8.4 illustrates the **fork/exec** process for the menu application.

In some applications, the parent process will not wait for the child process to die after a **fork**. For example, a word-processing program might print a document while allowing its user to continue editing another document. Figure 8.5 shows how this concurrent work can be accomplished. The **editor** program forks a child process, which execs the **printer** program to print the requested document. In this instance, the parent process continues to execute, allowing the user to edit other documents.

An Example: The Shell and Process Management

The XENIX shells use the XENIX process structure to carry out user commands. Very few commands are built into the shell itself. In fact, most commands are separate utility programs, independent of the shell. When the shell process receives a command, the following operations take place:

1. The shell process forks a child process to execute the command.
2. The child process execs the utility program named in the command. Now two processes are running for the user: the shell (parent) process and the utility (child) process.
3. If the command is to be run in the foreground, the shell process waits for its child process to complete. The utility program may interact with the user at the terminal without interference from the shell. When the child process terminates, the shell prompts the user for the next command.

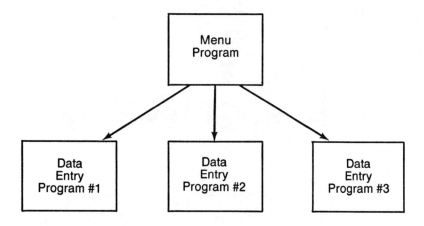

Fig. 8.3. A menu-driven application.

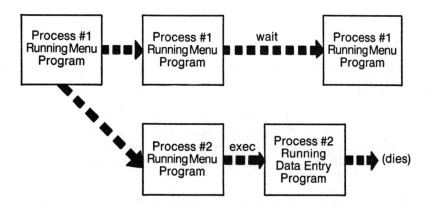

*Fig. 8.4. **fork** and **exec** in a menu-driven application.*

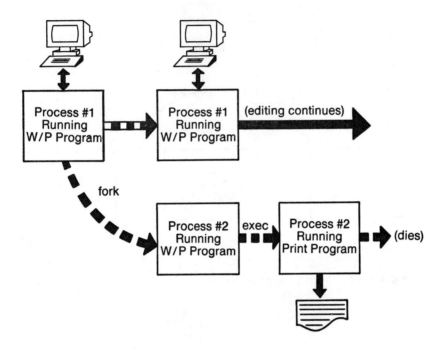

*Fig. 8.5. **fork** and **exec** in a word-processing application.*

4. If the user requests background execution of the command, the shell process does not wait for the child process. Instead, the shell process prints the process-id of the child process and immediately prompts for the next command.

The shell's use of the process mechanism gives each user the ability to perform several different tasks on the system at once. Each request for background processing simply results in a new child process of the shell process.

The Environment of a Process

Each process on a XENIX system is launched with an *environment*, consisting of a set of named variables. The process may access these variables and obtain their values during its execution. These *environment variables* are the shell variables described in Chapter 6, whose values have been made part of the environment through a shell command. A process retains its environment across an **exec** system call; a child process inherits its parent's environment as a result of a **fork** system call.

Effective User-Id's

A process normally executes with the user-id of the user who initiates it. This user-id determines the process's permission to access files on the system and the process's ability to make privileged system calls. A child process inherits its parent's user-id and, thus, the parent's permissions and privileges. Certain tasks, however, require that a process be able to execute with permissions and privileges that exceed those of its parent.

For example, suppose that payroll clerks will enter time-card data into a payroll file through a payroll data entry program. The payroll clerk should *not* have read access to the payroll file because it contains sensitive salary data. The data entry program, however, must have read access to the payroll file to verify correct data entry of employee numbers and other information. If the data entry program is executed simply on behalf of the data entry clerk, the program will not have the required read access permission.

XENIX solves this problem by allowing a process to execute with a user-id that is different from that of its parent. The process runs with an *effective user-id*, which is the user-id of the owner of the file containing the program, instead of the user-id of the parent process. Programs to be executed with an effective user-id are identified by a flag, which is stored with the ownership and permission information for the program file. This *set user-id* flag instructs the kernel to use an effective user-id when executing the program. A parallel *set group-id* flag causes the kernel to use an *effective group-id* when executing the program.

In the example, the payroll data entry program would be stored in a file whose owner had read access to the payroll file. The set user-id flag for the program would also be set. When the data entry clerk runs the program, it can successfully read the payroll file, even though the data entry clerk continues to be denied this access.

Extreme care must be taken to ensure that indiscriminate use of the effective user-id capability does not result in a breach of system security. Programs that set an effective user-id should be well debugged and severely limited in function.

File Sharing and Locking

The XENIX system allows a file to be accessed by many different programs at the same time. In an inventory control application, for example, several different programs may be reading data from an inventory master file, to retrieve price information in response to inventory part numbers typed by users.

A problem arises, however, if several programs attempt to share a file that will be updated or modified. For example, suppose two concurrent users are running a program that modifies quantity-on-hand data for parts in inventory. If both users attempt to modify the quantity-on-hand data for the same part at the same time, then the data in the file will not be updated correctly. Each user's program will first obtain the same quantity-on-hand data from the file, modify its value, and then place the modified data back into the file. However, only the second program to replace the data will have its change reflected in the file. The change made by the first program will simply be overwritten.

To permit correct concurrent update of files, XENIX includes a system call to implement a scheme known as *file locking*. Using the file-locking system call, an application program can *lock* a particular range of bytes in a file, temporarily reserving them for its own exclusive use. The program can then retrieve data from that part of the file, modify it, and replace it in the file, with the assurance that no other program may access the data at the same time. The section of the file is released with another system call that *unlocks* it. If a second application program attempts to access part of a file that is locked by the first program, the XENIX kernel causes the second program to wait, with its execution suspended until the first program unlocks that part of the file. The system call for file locking can be used to implement "record level" or even "item level" locking in an application.

XENIX offers an especially rich set of options to the file locking system call. A process can lock part of a file against both read and write access by other processes, or the process may permit reading while disallowing writing. Furthermore, a process that attempts to lock a region can choose to be either suspended until the region is free or immediately notified that the requested region is not available and that the lock has failed. Finally, the XENIX kernel itself provides protection against a *deadlock* condition, which occurs when each of two processes attempts to lock a region that has previously been locked by the other.

Device Sharing

Although XENIX files can be shared by several users simultaneously, some types of devices cannot be shared in this way. Examples include communications lines and floppy disks that are being used for backup operations. XENIX provides a mechanism that allows users to share these devices through the **assign** and **deassign** utilities.

A user requests exclusive access to a nonshareable device through the **assign** utility. If the exclusive access is granted, then other users will be denied access. When the user no longer needs the device, it is once again made available to other users with the **deassign** utility.

Process Scheduling*

In a multiprocessing environment, with many processes competing for time on a single CPU, the system must continually decide which process to work on next. This decision is called *scheduling*, and it is one of the main functions of the XENIX system kernel. The kernel schedules processes for execution according to a priority scheme. Each active process has an associated priority; the kernel selects the highest-priority process for execution each time the CPU becomes available.

A process's priority fluctuates, depending on the process's recent behavior. XENIX discriminates in favor of processes that are I/O-intensive by gradually raising their priority. XENIX discriminates against processes that are CPU-intensive by gradually lowering their priority. Thus, XENIX favors I/O-intensive processes that only need the CPU for a short time. CPU-intensive processes "fill in" when there are no I/O-intensive processes ready to execute. This scheduling scheme results in good average response times for users performing interactive (I/O-intensive) tasks; such an environment is typical for turnkey applications processing.

A process continues execution on the CPU until one of several events occurs. If the process performs an I/O operation or waits for some other system resource, the process will lose the CPU. A process will also lose the CPU after the process has executed for some fixed period of time (usually one second). This scheme prevents CPU-intensive processes from "hogging" the CPU, again ensuring good response times for interactive applications.

A user cannot improve the priority of his processes over other users' processes that are also executing on the system. Users can, however, *decrease* the priority of their processes with the **nlce** utility. This utility is typically used for CPU-intensive background processes, such as the XENIX text-formatting utilities.

Memory Management*

Active processes take up main memory space on a XENIX system; their instructions and data must be loaded into main memory for execution. When only a few processes are active, they may all fit into main memory together. The CPU can switch between processes very rapidly, and system response time will be very good.

On a busy XENIX system, however, all the active processes cannot fit into main memory at once. XENIX handles this situation by keeping only some of the active processes in main memory and the rest on the disk. Active processes are then shuttled between memory and disk, as the CPU switches from process to process, giving each active process its turn for execution. The task of arranging the processes in main memory and moving them to and from the disk is called *memory management*, which is a function of the XENIX kernel.

The memory management scheme used by the kernel is closely tied to the computer's hardware. Some CPUs, for example, require that an entire process be stored in one contiguous location in main memory. Other CPUs allow a process to be broken into pieces and scattered all over memory. Some CPUs require that an entire process be loaded into memory before the process can be executed. Others allow a process to execute with only a few pieces of the process in memory. The memory management function in the kernel must therefore be customized for each new computer system to which XENIX is ported.

Two major memory management techniques are used in the various versions of the UNIX system. The first, called *swapping*, is the traditional UNIX memory management scheme. XENIX has this technique. The second, called *virtual memory*, was first used in the Berkeley versions of the UNIX system. Both of these memory management schemes are described in detail in the following sections.

Process Swapping *

Swapping is the memory management technique used in current XENIX implementations. It requires that an entire process be present in main memory for execution.

Swapping shuttles entire processes between the memory and a reserved area of the disk, known as the *swap area*. When a process in main memory has received its share of the CPU's available time, the process is *swapped out* (copied to the swap area), and one or more of the active processes on the disk are *swapped in* (copied into main memory) so that the CPU can work on them.

Swapping diminishes the performance of the system, as perceived by each user. When swapping, the system must spend a small percentage of its time shuttling processes between disk and memory, which reduces the time available for actual process execution. But the overhead of swapping is ordinarily worth this inconvenience because swapping allows a XENIX system to run more processes than could otherwise fit into main memory at one time. The alternative is not to allow some of the processes to execute at all!

If the system attempts to work on many more processes than can fit into main memory at once, swapping can become a heavy burden. When the system spends a high percentage of its time on swapping, response time for interactive users will increase dramatically. (This phenomenon is known as *thrashing*.) There are two alternatives to remedy this problem: reduce the load on the system by moving some users to other machines, or purchase more memory so that more processes can fit into main memory at one time.

To maximize swapping's efficiency, the kernel uses a dedicated area on the disk for this technique. A copy of each process is made in this swap area when the process is first started, and the copy is updated each time the process is swapped out. The process image is removed from the swap area when the process dies, making room for the swapping of other processes. Even if the program is requested again a few seconds later, a fresh copy of it must be created in the swap area.

*The Sticky Bit**

On a typical XENIX system, a handful of utility programs account for the vast majority of the commands executed by users. Constantly reloading these programs into the swap area for execution becomes a drain on system performance, especially if the programs are large. The system administrator can instruct XENIX to keep permanent copies of these frequently executed programs in the swap area. This instruction is given by setting the program file's *sticky bit*, a flag stored with the ownership and access permissions for the file.

When a program's sticky bit is set, its process image remains permanently in the swap area, even after the process dies. On subsequent executions, the program can be loaded very quickly because the process image is already in the swap area. In a system used for program development, likely candidates for the sticky bit are the shell, the editor, and the C compiler. In a turnkey system, the most heavily used data entry and inquiry programs are candidates for the sticky bit.

Virtual Memory*

Some newer computer systems feature memory management hardware that does not require an entire process to be loaded into memory in order to execute it. Instead, the CPU can execute a process with only a part of the process loaded. If the CPU attempts to execute a part of the process that is not loaded, the hardware detects this condition, and the operating system brings the missing part into memory. The technique of breaking an active process into pieces, which are brought into main memory only as they are needed, is called *virtual memory*.

Virtual memory hardware is available on most superminicomputers and mainframes. It is also available on the new generation of advanced microprocessors, such as the Motorola M68010, the Intel iAPX 286, and the National Semiconductor 16032. The Berkeley versions of the UNIX system include software support for virtual memory operation. Microcomputer ports of UNIX with virtual memory support are just beginning to appear. XENIX does not yet support virtual memory, but it is a likely enhancement for future XENIX versions.

Virtual memory has two major benefits. It allows a system to execute very large programs, even those that are many times larger than the available main memory on the system. Virtual memory can also be more efficient than swapping because portions of a greater number of processes can be retained in main memory at the same time.

Interprocess Communications*

Many applications are most conveniently implemented as a family of cooperating processes. For example, a data base inquiry application may be built with a "front-end" process that interacts with the user and a "back-end server" process, which accesses the data base. Such applications rely on the kernel to provide process-to-process communications services that tie the individual processes into a single application.

XENIX offers several tools for process-to-process communications. The oldest and most widely used tool is the UNIX pipe. An enhanced form of the pipe, known as a *named pipe*, was introduced in UNIX

System III and is included in current versions of XENIX. XENIX has added still more advanced interprocess communications capabilities through *shared memory* and *semaphores.*

Pipes*

Recall from Chapter 6 that the shell uses pipes to connect programs in a sequence, sending the standard output of one program to the standard input of the next. Actually, pipes are not a feature of the shell but rather a service provided by the kernel. Pipes can be used by applications programs to send messages from one process to another.

A pipe is a one-way communication path between processes. The *sending* process puts messages into the pipe, and the *receiving* process removes them. The pipe is perceived by each process to be an ordinary file. If two-way communication is required, two pipes are used, one for message traffic in each direction.

The kernel manages a pipe on a first-in-first-out basis. The sending process places data into the pipe with the standard **write** system call. The kernel holds the data until the receiving process requests the data with the standard **read** system call. Data is supplied to the receiving process in exactly the same order in which the data was placed into the pipe by the sending process. Figure 8.6 shows two processes connected by a pipe.

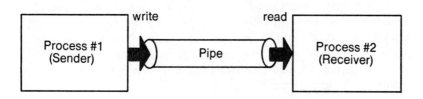

Fig. 8.6. The XENIX pipe feature.

Typically, the processes connected by a pipe will send and receive data at different rates. The kernel automatically synchronizes the sending and receiving processes, forcing the sending process to wait if the pipe becomes full, and forcing the receiving process to wait if the pipe becomes empty. Synchronization is completely transparent to the programs themselves.

Pipes are limited by the requirement that both the sending and receiving processes have a common parent process. A new form of pipe, called a named pipe, addresses this limitation. With named pipes, two unrelated processes can communicate.

*Nonblocking Reads**

Normally, a process reading data from a pipe or terminal is suspended if no data is available. The process will wait indefinitely, until another process places data in the pipe or a user types characters on the terminal keyboard. In some applications this suspension is desired. For example, a data base server process reading from a pipe should wait—possibly for minutes or hours—until a request for service arrives. For other applications, however, this loss of control while waiting for an external event is unacceptable.

The XENIX *nonblocking read* capability allows a process to retain control over its own operation while reading data from a pipe or terminal. With nonblocking reads, if no data is currently available, a process's request to read data simply returns immediately. The process can then proceed with other work and try to read data again at a later time. A process must explicitly request nonblocking reads when the file is first opened.

Nonblocking reads are a key feature for certain types of applications. For example, in a communications application a communication line may fail, with the result that no data comes into the system. The process responsible for receiving incoming data must be able to detect this condition and act on it, instead of waiting indefinitely for data to appear. Nonblocking reads provide this capability.

Shared Memory*

Although pipes offer a simple mechanism for communication between processes, pipes move data very slowly, compared to the
speed of memory-to-memory data transfers within a process.
Higher-performance interprocess communication is available
through the XENIX shared memory facility. With shared memory, a
portion of the system's main memory, called a shared data segment,
is made available for sharing among multiple processes. Each process views the shared data segment as if it were a part of the process's own data area. Data placed in the shared data segment by
one process is immediately accessible to all other processes. The
processes are thus closely linked, and interprocess communication
is very fast. Figure 8.7 illustrates shared memory operation.

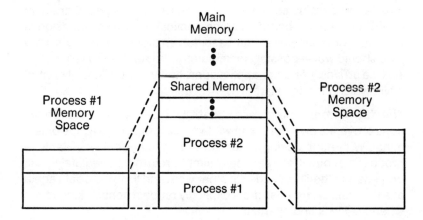

Fig. 8.7. Shared memory operation.

The processes using a shared data segment coordinate their access to it through a set of XENIX system calls. A pair of calls is used
to request and relinquish exclusive access to the shared data segment. XENIX also maintains a version number for the shared data
segment. This number is automatically incremented each time a
process requests exclusive access. Other processes can monitor

the version number to detect updates to the data in the shared data segment.

Shared memory not only allows interprocess communication, but also supports concurrent access to common data by separate processes. This access is a key requirement for certain types of on-line applications. In an airline reservation system, for example, multiple processes can use shared memory to maintain a table of available seats, ensuring that each process has access to the same up-to-date information.

Semaphores*

Semaphores provide a general-purpose tool for sharing resources among multiple processes. For an example of the use of semaphores, consider the application in figure 8.8. Two processes are printing messages on the same system printer. If the two processes send output to the printer at approximately the same time, then the characters of their messages may become intermixed.

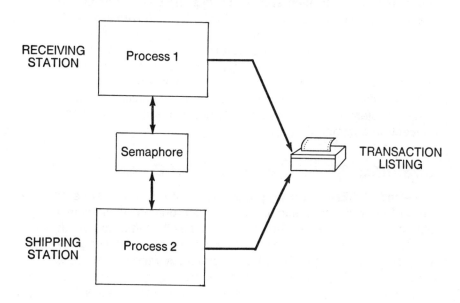

Fig. 8.8. Semaphore operation.

The processes can coordinate their access to the printer by using the XENIX *semaphore* mechanism. Before the first process prints its message, the process locks a semaphore to obtain exclusive access to the printer. If the second process attempts to lock the semaphore before the first process unlocks it, then the second process will be suspended. The second process will resume its execution only after the first process unlocks the semaphore. In this way, each process can print its complete messages to the printer, without interference from the other. Semaphores are used through a set of XENIX system calls.

Building a Turnkey Application

XENIX provides applications designers with a modular system structure that can be easily customized to meet specific applications requirements. The XENIX start-up procedures can be tailored to place the system automatically into an applications processing mode without user intervention. The login procedure can be modified to perform application-specific processing before admitting a user to the system. The standard XENIX shells can be replaced with an alternative user interface that prompts and guides the user through application choices. Applications can be insulated from terminal dependencies. Finally, programs can be automatically executed at specified times without manual intervention. In short, the XENIX system can be transformed into a turnkey applications processing system, whose users have no need to understand XENIX concepts or commands.

Customizing the Start-up Procedures

The standard XENIX start-up procedure executes a sequence of four XENIX utilities to create a multiuser environment. Immediately after the system is booted, the kernel launches the **init** utility, which initializes the system and prepares it to accept user logins. The **getty** utility displays the login prompt on a terminal screen and accepts the user name. The **login** utility validates the user name and password and starts the shell to accept commands from the user. When a user logs out, the shell process terminates, and the **init** process is responsible for starting the login procedure all over again. Figure

8.9 illustrates the start-up sequence and the relationships between the utility programs that comprise it.

At the beginning of the start-up sequence, the **init** utility offers an opportunity to place the system in a special *maintenance mode* before continuing the start-up sequence to full multiuser operation. Maintenance mode is used for system backup and other administrative functions that require single user operation. In maintenance mode, the user has super-user capabilities. The root password must therefore be supplied before maintenance mode is entered, thus preserving system security.

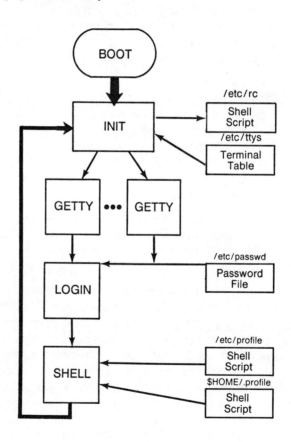

Fig. 8.9. XENIX start-up sequence.

The **init** utility next executes the file **/etc/rc** as a shell script. This script usually performs file system checks, purges temporary files, mounts file systems, starts system accounting, and so on. The script may be modified to customize the start-up sequence. Finally, **init** reads the file **/etc/ttys**, which contains a list of the serial communications lines connected to the system, and opens each one as specified.

In standard multiuser operation, **init** spawns one child process per terminal. Each of these child processes executes the **getty** utility, which displays the login prompt, accepts the user name, and executes the **login** utility. The **login** utility verifies the user name and password against the list of authorized users stored in the **/etc/passwd** file. This file contains one entry per user. Each entry includes the following critical pieces of information:

- The user name
- The encrypted password
- The user-id
- The group-id to be used on login
- The real name of the user
- The name of the home directory
- The name of the program to be launched after successful login (usually the shell)

If login is successful, the **login** utility sets up the user-id and group-id and places the user in the user's home directory. Finally, the **login** utility execs the shell, marking successful completion of the login sequence.

Before displaying its prompt, the Bourne shell checks for two special *profile* files and executes them as shell scripts. The *system profile* script, stored in the file **/etc/profile**, typically prints the message of the day, checks for mail, and so on. This script can be modified to perform application-specific functions, as necessary. The *user profile* script, stored in the file named **.profile** in the user's home directory, performs user-specific functions, such as assigning values to shell variables. The C shell offers a similar capability through the profile scripts **.login** and **.cshrc**. The user can modify these scripts to customize the user's own start-up sequence.

If an application requires special security checking or other special login processing, the application designer can replace the **getty** and **login** utilities with programs of special design. For example, the designer can substitute programs that display a login form on the terminal screen or that download code into an intelligent terminal before operation.

Alternative User Interfaces

The standard XENIX system shells provide a good user interface for general-purpose processing on a XENIX system. When a XENIX-based computer system is dedicated to a particular application, however, an alternative user interface may be better suited to the needs of system users. For example, for turnkey applications processing, menu shells offer a simple method of providing a limited set of application choices to the user.

XENIX makes it simple for applications designers to replace the standard XENIX shells with an alternative user interface. For each user, the name of the program that is to be launched, following a successful login, is stored in the **/etc/passwd** file. Normally, this program is one of the standard XENIX shells. However, an alternative program may be specified simply by replacing the name of the standard shell with another program name.

Terminal-Independent Applications

A XENIX system may have many different kinds of terminals connected to it, each with different hardware and software characteristics. The **stty** utility is used to configure the XENIX system for operation with different types of terminals and communications protocols. The **termcap** facility is a set of routines and files that supports the development of applications programs which are independent of variations in terminal characteristics.

The **stty** utility informs the kernel of terminal and communications line characteristics. This utility is used to specify the data communications speed of the terminal (for example, 2,400 or 9,600 baud); whether parity checking will be performed; characters for backspacing and end-of-file; and similar characteristics. The kernel adapts to these characteristics, insulating applications programs from them.

In addition, screen-oriented applications programs need to perform control operations on a terminal, such as clearing the screen or moving the cursor to a particular position on the screen. The control codes that perform these functions vary from terminal to terminal. The **termcap** facility helps to insulate applications programs from these variations. The **/etc/termcap** file contains a table of terminal capabilities and control codes for commonly used terminals. Each entry in the table corresponds to a particular brand of terminal, identified by a name. For each user, the environment variable **TERM** is set to one of these terminal names, identifying the terminal brand for that user.

Often the **TERM** variable is set at the time of login by a command in the user's **.profile** script. The **tset** (terminal **set**) utility can be used to set automatically the proper terminal type. This utility uses the file **/etc/ttytype**, which contains a list of the serial I/O lines attached to the system and the type of terminal connected to each line.

To perform screen-oriented operations, an application program determines the name of the terminal by obtaining the value of the **TERM** variable, and uses **termcap** routines to obtain information about the terminal's characteristics from the **/etc/termcap** table. In this way, a single program can be used by all users of a XENIX system, despite variations in the terminals used. Figure 8.10 illustrates the use of the **termcap** facility.

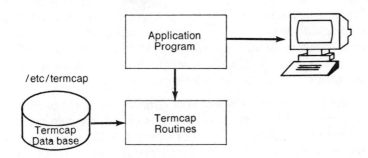

Fig. 8.10. Using the termcap facility.

The XENIX **curses** facility provides a high-level terminal interface built on **termcap**. **curses** is a library of screen input/output routines that manage an image of the terminal screen in main memory for an application program. The **curses** routines perform the following functions on the screen image:

- Move the cursor
- Insert and delete characters and lines
- Draw boxes, display character enhancements, etc.
- Create and manipulate sections of the screen, called *windows*
- Scroll sections of the screen image

After a set of manipulations to the screen image, **curses** updates the actual screen display on the program's behalf. The facility uses the **termcap** data base to update the screen in the most efficient manner for the particular type of terminal that is being used. Figure 8.11 illustrates the use of the **curses** routines.

The **curses** facility is useful for building full-screen applications. It insulates the programmer from the complex details of low-level screen management. Originally offered as part of the Berkeley UNIX system, **curses** is included as a standard part of XENIX.

Automatic Program Execution

Turnkey applications often include functions that must be performed repeatedly on a periodic basis. System backup, for example, may be performed each evening during nonworking hours to ensure easy recovery from any errors that may occur. Or an application may transmit a transaction file to a mainframe for processing twice a day, at regularly scheduled hours.

The XENIX utility **cron** can be used to perform automatically these periodic functions, without manual intervention by the system administrator or other users. A table stored in the file **/usr/lib/crontab** lists the programs to be periodically executed and the specific times when they are to be run. The **cron** utility reads this file and causes the programs to be executed as requested. Normally, the utility is started as a background process by the XENIX system start-up sequence and executes continuously. The system administrator is responsible for maintaining the **/usr/lib/crontab** file.

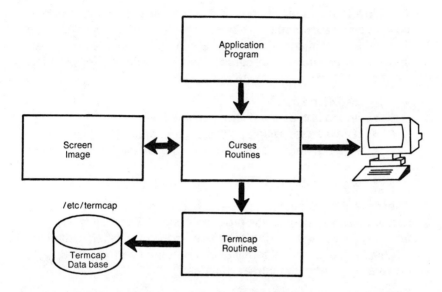

Fig. 8.11. Using the **curses** facility.

9

File Processing

Of over two hundred XENIX system utilities, a large number—perhaps the majority—are used to process text or data in files. These file-processing utilities offer the user a wide range of functions. Some utilities are particularly useful on text files; other utilities are designed to work on tabular data in the familiar row-column format. In typical XENIX style, each utility is specialized and designed to do one thing well. Taken as a group, the utilities give the user a powerful array of tools to manipulate file contents.

Many file-processing utilities are filters, each of which takes a single input file and processes its contents into a single output file. This action makes filters even more useful when they are combined in pipelines. A sequence of simple utilities can perform complex file-processing operations, eliminating the need to develop custom file-processing programs.

This chapter describes the general-purpose file-processing utilities. Those that have a more specialized use (for example, typesetting or program debugging) are described in the following chapters.

143

The following functions are available through the file-processing utilities:

- Splitting and combining files
- Comparing file contents
- Searching and modifying file contents
- Sorting and ordering file contents
- Manipulating tabular data
- Compressing and encrypting files

The command descriptions in this chapter include examples based on a **results** file whose contents are described in figure 9.1. The **results** file contains lines that represent individual sales orders. Each line consists of five fields that list, in order, the salesperson, the office, the region, the customer number, and the amount of the sale.

The **results** file contains a five-column table:

Jones	boston	east	0221349	60000
Jones	boston	east	0213412	57995
Davis	boston	east	0210497	4650
Harris	newyork	east	0491207	19425
Harris	newyork	east	0421007	30000
Andrews	phila	east	0412095	2950
salesperson	office	region	customer number	amount

Fig. 9.1. Contents of **results** file.

Combining and Splitting Files

Many applications require that information in different files be combined together or that a single large file be split into several smaller ones. For example, data from several different laboratory experiments may be stored in separate files, which must be combined for analysis. Chapters of a manuscript may be stored in different files, which must be combined to form a complete text. In another application, accounting transactions may be kept in a single large file, which must be split into smaller files for department-by-department expense reporting. In each of these examples, standard XENIX utilities can perform the file processing. Table 9.1 lists the utilities that split and combine files.

head	Copies text from the beginning of a file to the Compares two files, generating a side-by-side listing of their contents
tail	Copies text from the end of a file to the standard output
split	Divides a large file into a sequence of smaller files
csplit	Divides a file into sections (like **split**) but splits based on patterns in the file
cat	Combines the contents of several files into one large file

Table 9.1. Utilities That Split and Combine Files

Combining Files with *cat*

Perhaps the most frequently used file-processing utility is **cat** (con-**cat**enate files), which combines the contents of several files into a single file. The files to be combined are named in sequence on the command line:

```
$ cat boston/results newyork/results
.
.
.
```

The **cat** utility copies the contents of the first file to the standard output, followed by contents of the second file, and so on, until all the files have been copied. This process is illustrated in figure 9.2. If there is only one file in the list, the **cat** utility simply copies the contents of the file to the standard output. This copying is often done in order to list a file's contents on a terminal. The command

```
$ cat boston/results newyork/results phila/results > results
.
.
.
```

is used in conjunction with output redirection, to store the contents of several files in a single output file.

Splitting Files with *split* and *csplit*

The **split** and **csplit** utilities are the opposite of **cat**. They take a single large file and divide it into several smaller ones. Figure 9.3 illustrates the operation of these utilities. The **split** utility divides a file into files with equal numbers of lines, regardless of the file's contents. This utility can be used, for example, to divide a file of 10,000 lines into ten files of 1,000 lines each, which can then be more easily edited.

The **csplit** utility gives the user more control over how the file is split. A series of *patterns*, given on the command line, is matched against the lines in the input file. The **csplit** utility copies lines from the input file into an output file and starts a new output file each time the next pattern specified on the command line is matched. For example, the **results** file in figure 9.1 contains sales results for all the eastern region sales offices, sorted in order by office. Each line of the file contains the name of the office from which the sale was made. The command

```
$ csplit results /newyork/ /phila/
180
120
60
$ ▮
```

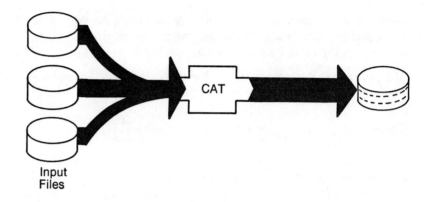

*Fig. 9.2. Concatenating files with **cat**.*

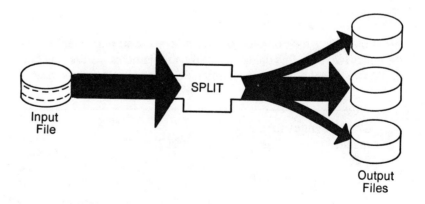

*Fig. 9.3. Splitting files with **split**.*

creates a separate output file containing the results for each sales office and prints out the number of bytes contained in each output file. More complex splits are also possible.

Other utilities in this group include **head** and **tail**, which select only the beginning or end of a file for processing.

Comparing and Contrasting Files

It is often useful to compare the contents of two files to see if they are the same, or if they are not, to determine the nature of their differences. For example, a user may make a copy of a critical file and then want to compare it to the original to be certain that the copy was made correctly. Or a user may have two files, one containing quarter-to-date sales transactions and the other containing month-to-date transactions. The user may want to obtain the differences in the two files, to get a list of transactions up to, but not including, the current month. In another example, a user who has been interrupted while editing a file may have forgotten exactly which changes were made. Comparing the "before editing" file with the "after editing" file gives a quick list of the changes. Standard XENIX utilities can be used for these and other file comparison functions. Table 9.2 lists some of these utilities.

Comparing Files

A simple utility for comparing files is **cmp** (**comp**are). Given the names of two files, this utility compares them and prints the position in the two files where they first differ. For example, the command

```
$ cmp results1 results2
results1 results2 differ: char 28, line 2
$ ▋
```

indicates that the two files first differ at the twenty-eighth character position, which occurs on the second line of the file. If the files are identical, then **cmp** prints nothing. Figure 9.4 illustrates the operation of **cmp**.

cmp	Compares two files, either reporting that they are identical or giving the position where they first differ
comm	Compares two sorted files, reporting on lines that are common to both, lines that appear only in the first file, and lines that appear only in the second file
sdiff	Compares two files, generating a side-by-side listing of their contents
diff	Compares two files and generates a list of the actions that are required to edit the first file so that it is identical to the second file
diff3	Compares three files and generates a list of their differences
dircmp	Compares directories and generates various tabulated information about their contents
sum	Computes a checksum based on the contents of a file
wc	Counts the number of lines, words, and characters in a file

Table 9.2. File Comparison Utilities

More information on file differences is provided by the **comm** and **sdiff** utilities. The **comm** utility takes two sorted files, compares them, and generates a three-column output report. The first column lists lines that appear only in the first file, the second column lists lines that appear only in the second file, and the third column lists lines that appear in both files. The **sdiff** utility produces an alternative two-column report, where lines from the two files are listed side by side. A one-character column between the side-by-side listings labels each line as unique to one file, unique to the other, or identical in both files.

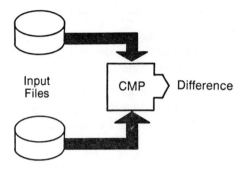

Input Files   CMP   Difference

Fig. 9.4. Comparing files with **cmp**.

Contrasting Files

Often users will want to compare two versions of the same file, one of which is an edited version of the other. The **diff** utility, as well as several others, is used for this kind of comparison. The output of the **diff** utility is a list of editing actions; when applied to the contents of the first file, these actions will generate the second, edited file. Editing actions include adding a line, deleting a line, or changing a line.

An option to the **diff** command causes output to be generated in the form of actual commands for the XENIX text editor (described in Chapter 10). With this option the user can store only an original file, plus a short sequence of editor commands produced by the **diff** utility. These commands can be applied to the original file to re-create a later version of the file whenever it is needed. If the files are large and the differences between them are minor, this method can be very efficient in storing different versions of the same file on a XENIX system.

Word Counts and Checksums

A simple utility named **wc** (**w**ord **c**ount) counts and prints the number of lines, words, and characters in a file. If the file contains a list of items, such as a list of sales personnel, the **wc** utility offers an easy way to count the number of items in the list. This utility is frequently used in pipelines to count the number of items produced by the preceding command. For example, the pipeline

```
$ ls | wc -l
12
$ ▮
```

counts the number of files in the current directory by counting the lines in the output of the **ls** command. (The option **-l** instructs **wc** to count lines only.) The **wc** utility is yet another method for determining that two files are not identical, by discovering that they do not contain the same number of lines, words, or characters.

Another utility, named **sum** (check**sum**), calculates and prints a checksum on the contents of a file. A *checksum* is a number that results from arithmetically adding the contents of each computer word in the file. Two identical files will have the same checksum. It is unlikely that two nonidentical files will have the same checksum. Thus, two files with the same checksum have a high probability of being identical.

Searching and Modifying File Contents

A common file-processing operation is searching the contents of a file for a particular piece of information. For example, a sales manager may want to search the forecast file for all orders forecast by a particular salesperson, to focus special attention on that person. In another application, an accounts receivable file may be searched, listing out all accounts with outstanding balances older than sixty days. Or perhaps a set of files containing the text of several contracts must be searched for a particular clause or phrase.

Standard XENIX file-processing utilities can easily perform these kinds of searching and modifying tasks. File-searching utilities offer some of the most complex processing functions of all the file-processing utilities. These utilities can search a file for lines that match one or more patterns and then undertake a complex series of actions when matching lines are found in the file. Despite their ability to handle complex operations, file-searching utilities are most often used in fairly simple ways, as illustrated in the examples that follow. Table 9.3 summarizes the file-searching and modification utilities.

file	Makes intelligent guesses as to the contents of a file
grep	Searches an input file for lines that match a pattern and copies them to the standard output file
sed	Applies a set of user-specified editing commands to one or more input files
awk	Searches an input file for lines that match one of a set of patterns and performs a user-specified action for each pattern matched
dd	Performs common transformations on one or more input files, to produce an output file
tr	Passes through a file, character by character, selectively replacing or deleting characters

Table 9.3. Utilities That Search and Modify a File

File Searching with grep

The **grep** (**g**lobal **r**egular **e**xpression **p**rint) utility is the standard file-searching and selection utility. Figure 9.5 shows how it operates. The user specifies a pattern to guide **grep**'s search through a file. This utility examines the input file, line by line, checking each one to see if it contains the pattern. When a match is found, the line is copied to the standard output file. If a line does not contain the pattern, the line is not copied to the output file. When **grep** has completed its search, the output file contains the input file's lines that contain the pattern.

For example, to search the file **results** for sales from the Boston sales office, the user would type the following command:

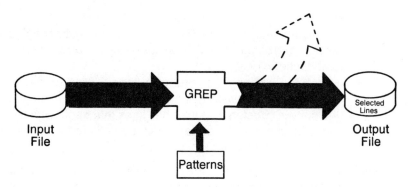

*Fig. 9.5. Searching files with **grep**.*

```
$ grep boston results
Jones      boston      east      0221349      60000
Jones      boston      east      0213412      57995
Davis      boston      east      0210497       4650
$ ■
```

The **grep** utility copies to the standard output only the lines that contain the word "boston" somewhere in each line.

The **grep** utility also acts as a filter in a pipeline. When used in a pipeline, **grep** selects some of the output of the preceding program for subsequent processing by the next program in the pipeline.

The patterns used by the **grep** utility are called *regular expressions* (hence, the strange name of the command). The flexible pattern-matching features of **grep** provide the following capabilities:

- Match any single character in a particular position, by including the wild-card character *dot* (.)
- Match a specific set of characters in a particular position, by enclosing the characters in *square brackets* (for example, **[abc]**)
- Match zero or more occurrences of a character, by following it with an *asterisk* (*). (For example, the pattern **abc*** matches the strings *ab, abccc, abccccc,* etc.)
- Match a bounded range of occurrences of a character, by enclosing the upper and lower bounds in *braces*. (For ex-

ample, the pattern **abc{4,7}** matches any string that begins with *ab* and continues with from four to seven occurrences of the letter *c*.)

- Match the beginning or end of a line, using the special characters *circumflex* (^) and *dollar sign* ($). (For example, the pattern ^**boston** only matches lines that begin with the word *boston*, and the pattern **boston$** only matches lines that end with the word.)

Options to the **grep** utility permit the user to select lines that do *not* match the pattern, to output only the line numbers of the lines that match, and so on. The **grep** utility can also read its patterns from a file rather than from the command line. This feature is useful for handling complex patterns.

More Complex Pattern Matching with *awk*

The **grep** utility provides sophisticated pattern-matching capability but a limited choice of actions for lines that match the patterns. Each line of the input file is either placed or not placed in the output file; no further processing of the line is performed. The **awk** utility extends pattern-matching processing much further. This utility, therefore, can be used as a sophisticated report-writing tool.

Like **grep**, the **awk** utility passes through a file, line by line, attempting to match each line to a set of patterns. But for each pattern, **awk** allows the user to specify what *action* is to be taken when a line that matches the pattern is encountered. The user may instruct the **awk** utility to scan through the **results** file, searching for lines that contain sales from the eastern region, printing column headers, accumulating total orders, and adding the cumulative total to the end of each line as it is sent to the output file.

Figure 9.6 shows how the **awk** utility operates. The patterns that control **awk**'s operation can be specified on the command line, or they can be stored in a file. For each pattern, the user also specifies a corresponding action.

The **awk** utility considers each line in the input file to be made up of one or more *fields*, which are separated by one or more blanks. Each field can be individually referenced, both in the patterns and in the actions. The patterns used by **awk** are like those described for

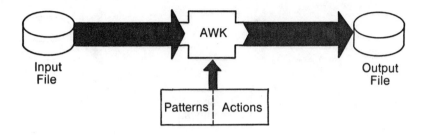

*Fig. 9.6. Pattern matching with **awk**.*

the **grep** utility in the preceding section. The actions taken form the basis of a comprehensive report-writing language with the following capabilities:

- Variable assignment and arithmetic computation
- Copying fields from the input line to the output file
- Sending formatted output to the output file
- Conditional testing **(if...then...else)**
- Looping **(while...do)**
- Iteration **(for...next)**

A detailed description of **awk**'s processing capabilities is beyond the scope of this text. The utility's notation is cryptic and difficult for a novice to understand. Yet the amount of processing that can be expressed with just a few lines is amazing. A C language program that performs the same processing might contain over a hundred lines of source code. A COBOL or Pascal program would be at least that long. In the hands of an experienced user, **awk** is a powerful and efficient report-generating tool that reduces the need for developing new file-processing programs.

File Editing with **sed**

Another pattern-matching utility with powerful processing capabilities is **sed** (**s**tream **ed**itor). The **sed** utility is an "automatic" version of the XENIX text editor **ed**, described in Chapter 10. Figure 9.7 illustrates **sed**'s operation.

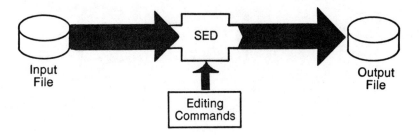

Fig. 9.7. Editing files with **sed**.

The **sed** utility reads lines, one by one, from an input file and applies a set of editing commands to the lines. The edited lines are then sent to the standard output file. The **sed** editing commands take exactly the same form as commands to the **ed** utility. However, **sed** operates on only a single line at a time and can be used to edit files that are too large for the **ed** text editor.

The editing commands used with **sed** include a pattern-matching capability like the one offered by **grep** and **awk**. But the **sed** editing commands offer more flexibility in adding, deleting, modifying, and searching lines of the input file as it is processed. In addition, **sed** can copy lines from the input file into a "holding buffer" and copy them to new positions in the output file. This utility can also merge lines from other files into the output file. The **sed** editing commands may be specified on the command line or stored in a file.

Sorting Files

Often the contents of a file must be sorted into some order before useful processing can proceed. The **sort** utility performs this function. The utility takes lines from one or more input files and sorts them, producing a standard output file containing the lines in sorted order. With **sort**, each line from an input file is treated as a series of one or more fields, separated from one another by spaces. The **sort** utility can reorder the file based on one or more of the fields.

For example, the **results** file may be sorted in order by the amount of each sale, for sales analysis. The command

```
$ sort +4nr results
Jones      boston     east      0221349   60000
Jones      boston     east      0213412   57995
Harris     newyork    east      0421007   30000
Harris     newyork    east      0491207   19425
Davis      boston     east      0210497   4650
Andrews    phila      east      0412095   2950
$ ■
```

will do the job. The **+4** on the command line instructs **sort** to skip the first four fields and sort on the fifth (amount) field. The **n** identifies the field as numeric, and the **r** instructs **sort** to reverse the sorting order so that the sales with the largest amounts appear first.

Additional options to the **sort** utility instruct it to sort based on multiple fields, merge multiple files, and perform other sophisticated processing. Other utilities are available to perform further sorting and ordering of functions, as shown in table 9.4.

sort	Sorts the lines of one or more files into order, using one or more sort keys
uniq	Finds and eliminates duplicate lines in a file and is often used with **sort**
nl	Produces an output file by inserting the line number of each line of an input file at the beginning of each line
tsort	Accepts as input a partial ordering and produces a fully ordered list of the items
look	Finds all lines in a sorted file that begin with a given string

Table 9.4. Utilities That Sort and Order a File

Processing Tabular Data

It is often useful to organize information in a file as a *table*, with the data neatly arranged into rows and columns. Each *row* of the table is stored as one line in the file. Each *column* in a row is stored as one field in the line, separated from adjacent columns by one or more spaces. The **results** file is an example of such a table. Several utilities previously described in this chapter are useful with tabular files. For example, the **sort** utility is convenient for sorting the rows of a table into order, based on the contents of one or more columns. The **grep** utility is also useful in selecting only certain rows of a table, for further processing, as illustrated in figure 9.8. Table 9.5 lists several additional utilities that are uniquely well suited for row-column processing on tabular files.

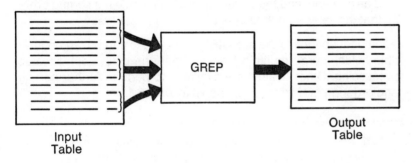

*Fig. 9.8. Selecting rows with **grep**.*

cut	Deletes columns from a file, producing a new file with shorter lines
paste	Combines the columns of two or more files, producing one file with longer lines that include all the columns in the original files
join	Combines corresponding lines in two files by relating the contents of one or more columns

Table 9.5. Utilities That Process Tabular (Row-Column) Data

Projecting Columns with cut

The **cut** utility deletes columns from a table. For instance, suppose a user wanted to project from the **results** file only the columns containing the salesrep, the customer number, and the sale amount. The command

```
$ cut -f1,4,5 results
Jones      0221349           60000
Jones      0213412      57995
Davis      0210497      4650
Harris     0491207      19425
Harris     0421007      30000
Andrews    0412095      2950
$ ■
```

will select these columns (identified as the first, fourth, and fifth fields, with the option **-f1,4,5** on the command line). The specified columns are copied to the standard output file. Figure 9.9 illustrates the action of **cut**.

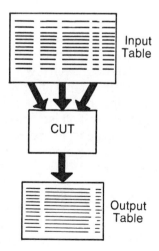

*Fig. 9.9. Projecting columns with **cut**.*

Combining Tables with *paste*

The **paste** utility takes two tables and combines them, side by side, to form a single wide table as output. The lines of the input files must therefore be in corresponding order before the **paste** utility can be used. This utility is the opposite of **cut**. Figure 9.10 illustrates the action of *paste*.

Note that the **paste** utility expands a table's width, increasing the number of columns. The **cat** utility, previously described in this chapter, expands a table's length, increasing the number of rows.

Relating Tables with *join*

The **join** utility combines data from two tables that contain related information. For example, suppose that the **results** file is to be augmented by adding the name of the appropriate sales office manager to each line of the file. A second file, named **office**, holds a table of sales offices and office managers in two columns:

newyork	**Johnson**
boston	**Anderson**
phila	**Smith**

The **join** utility can be used to create the desired file, matching rows from the two tables, based on the field that is common to both (in this example, the sales office). For each row in the **results** table, the corresponding row in the **office** table (the row with the same sales office) is located. An output row is then created, containing all the columns of the first table and all the columns of the second table. Options to the **join** utility allow the user to choose only certain columns from each table for inclusion in the output table. Figure 9.11 illustrates the action of **join**.

The **join** utility is a powerful tool for cross-referencing data from file to file. To process files for reporting, this utility is often used with the **cut**, **paste**, **sort**, **split**, and **grep** utilities. These utilities, in fact, implement the features of a relational data base management system for processing tabular files. The relational *selection* operation is implemented by the **grep** utility. The *projection* operation is implemented

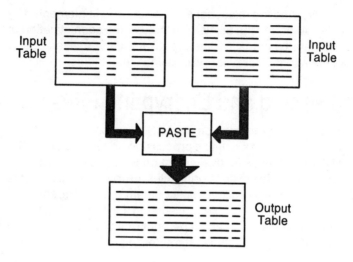

*Fig. 9.10. Combining tables with **paste**.*

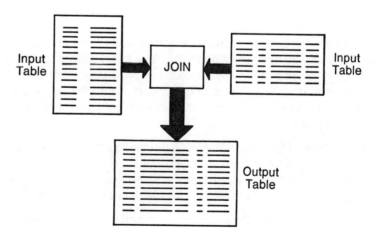

*Fig. 9.11. Relating tables with **join**.*

by the **cut** utility. And the relational *join* operation is implemented by the **join** utility. Although the utilities fall short of the sophistication of commercial data base management packages, the utilities offer a convenient relational facility for processing small tables.

Compressing and Encrypting Files

Generally, data files are stored on the XENIX system as plain ASCII text. This storing method simplifies processing because many of the XENIX utilities are most effectively used on text files or on files organized as tables. However, storing files in this manner wastes space. In particular, files will typically contain many sequences of blanks, with each blank character consuming a byte of disk storage. It is not unusual for as much as 30 percent of a file's storage to be consumed in storing these blank characters.

The **pack** utility compacts a file into less disk space by encoding its contents. The details of how files are compressed are not important here, only that a file's storage requirements will usually be reduced significantly by packing. Once a file has been packed, however, its contents will be unintelligible to the standard XENIX utilities. A companion utility, **unpack**, returns the file to its original state. Packing is normally used on extremely large files that are infrequently used, because unpacking the files for use can be a time-consuming operation.

If the contents of a file are especially sensitive, an extra measure of security is offered by encrypting the file. The **crypt** utility encodes a file's contents. The utility uses a user-supplied encryption key to transform the input file, character by character, into the coded output file. To reconstruct the original, uncoded data, the **crypt** utility decodes the output file.

As with a packed file, the coded file is unintelligible to the standard XENIX utilities. As a result, encoding is usually reserved for files that are used infrequently or for occasions when security is extremely critical, because encoded files must first be decoded for processing.

Table 9.6 describes the data compression and encryption utilities.

crypt	Encodes a file's contents, using a user-supplied encryption key, and decodes encrypted files
makekey	Generates an encryption key for use in programs that must perform encoding/decoding
pack	Generates a "packed" version of a file, which takes less disk space
pcat	Concatenates the contents of several packed files (like the **cat** utility)
unpack	Reconstructs the contents of the original file from a file that has been packed

Table 9.6. File Compression and Encryption Utilities

dosdir	Displays directory information in the format displayed by the MS-DOS **dir** command
dosls	Displays directory information in the format displayed by the XENIX **ls** command
doscat	Displays the contents of one or more files
doscp	Copies files
dosrm	Removes files
dosmkdir	Creates new directories
dosrmdir	Removes directories

Table 9.7. MS-DOS Interface Utilities

Processing MS-DOS Files

XENIX includes a set of MS-DOS interface utilities that permit limited processing of MS-DOS files under XENIX. These utilities can be used to access data stored on MS-DOS-formatted floppy disks. The utilities can also be used on XENIX systems where a separate MS-DOS partition exists on a hard disk. Table 9.7 lists the MS-DOS interface utilities.

10

Text Processing and Office Support

The XENIX system provides a comprehensive set of tools for document preparation and office automation. XENIX text-processing utilities support creation, editing, and formatting of documents. These documents may include text, tabular data, and even mathematical equations. Other utilities support personal office tasks, such as messaging, appointment scheduling, and calculation.

The strong XENIX emphasis on text processing is not surprising because one of the earliest applications of UNIX within the Bell System was document preparation. Another major application of UNIX has been software development, which also requires strong text-processing tools. It has been said (only partially in jest) that the UNIX system is really nothing but a very complicated text processor. This chapter describes the XENIX utilities that support text processing and office automation.

Text-Processing and Office Automation Facilities

XENIX supports text processing and office automation through a group of approximately thirty utility programs, which include the following:

- *Text editors*. The standard XENIX system includes both a line editor and a full-screen editor; other editors and word processors have been developed by third parties over the years.
- *Text formatters*. These tools transform text prepared with the XENIX text editors into formatted documents, such as letters, manuscripts, and manuals. The text-formatting tools work with a range of printing devices, from draft-quality printers to phototypesetters.
- *Text-processing aids*. XENIX utilities aid in hyphenation, produce indexes, and perform other text-processing functions.
- *Writing aids*. These utilities correct spelling errors and analyze writing style.
  Calculators. XENIX utilities simulate calculators with advanced features, such as memory registers, programmability, and programming language constructs.
- *Electronic mail*. An electronic mail facility lets users send messages to other users. Mail can be sent between users on the same system or across the telephone network to users of other systems.
- *Calendar services*. A calendar facility provides appointment tracking and reminder services that adapt to different styles of appointment scheduling.

Text-Processing Tools

The XENIX text-processing tools are a family of utilities that aid in all phases of document preparation. Figure 10.1 shows the phases of the document preparation process.

The XENIX text editors are used to enter the text of a document into the system and store it as a file. The same editors are later used to

Text Entry and Editing   Text Formatting and Printing

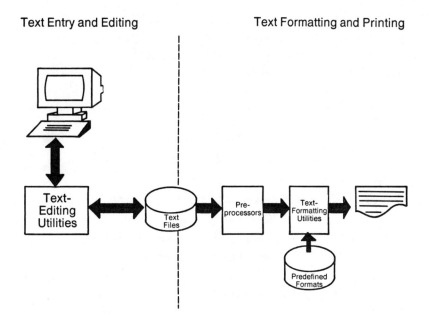

Fig. 10.1. Text processing with XENIX.

revise the document by adding, modifying, and deleting text. The two most popular XENIX editing utilities are **ed**, a line-oriented editor, and **vi**, a screen-oriented editor.

When a document is ready for printing, the XENIX text-formatting utilities control its appearance on the printed page. Formatting commands, included in the text file itself, direct how the unformatted text will be formed into paragraphs, pages, and sections of a document. The **nroff** utility formats text for printing on typewriter-like printing devices, such as draft-quality printers, letter-quality printers, and line printers.

A companion utility, **troff**, formats text for printing on high-resolution printing devices, for example, phototypesetters and laser printers. Other utilities handle specialized formatting tasks, such as printing tables and mathematical equations. These latter utilities are used as preprocessors to the main formatting programs.

Many of the file-processing commands described in the previous chapter are useful in combination with the text-editing and text-formatting utilities. The same utilities used to process tables of sales data, for example, can be applied equally well to files containing pages of a technical manual. Table 10.1 lists the most commonly used XENIX text-processing utilities.

ed	Edits a text file, using line-oriented editing
vi	Edits a text file, using screen-oriented editing
pr	Prints a text file with simple headers and page breaks
nroff	Formats text for printing on character-oriented printing devices
troff	Formats text for printing on high-resolution printing devices
tbl	Formats tabular data
eqn	Formats mathematical text and equations
cw	Formats text in a typewriter-style font for printing on high-resolution printing devices
mm	Formats common office documents, such as letters and memoranda
mmt	Formats text for viewgraphs
deroff	Removes formatting commands from a text file
hyphen	Finds hyphenated words in a text file
diffmk	Compares two versions of a file and produces a version with "change bars"
ptx	Produces a permuted index
spell	Corrects spelling errors

Table 10.1. (Continued on next page)

style	Analyzes readability of text
diction	Finds awkward phrases in text
explain	Suggests alternatives to awkward phrases in text

Table 10.1. Text-Processing Utilities

The XENIX Line Editor

The **ed** (**ed**itor) utility is the standard XENIX text editor. This utility is a *command-oriented* editor—it accepts editing commands from the user and performs the requested editing operations on the contents of a text file. The **ed** utility is also *line-oriented*. Its editing commands operate on a single line at a time or a range of lines. This text editor is useful for editing documents and other kinds of text stored in XENIX files.

A user's interaction with **ed** takes the form of a dialog. Like the shell, **ed** prompts the user for a command, accepts it, and carries it out before asking the user for the next command. During an editing session, **ed** stores the text being edited in an *editing buffer* in main memory. If an existing file is to be edited, its contents are first read from the disk into the buffer. When editing is complete, **ed** places the edited text from the buffer back onto the disk.

The editing commands available with **ed** offer a variety of editing functions, such as adding and deleting lines of text, changing text throughout a document, and moving lines of text from one position to another. Editing commands take the form of a single character. For example, the **p** command prints lines of text on the terminal display, and the **m** command moves a group of lines. Table 10.2 lists the most commonly used commands.

Each editing command operates on a single line or on a range of lines. The user selects the lines to be affected by each command. For example, the user may request that each occurrence of the word *Jim* be changed to *James* in lines 2 through 24 of a document. The user can also use pattern matching and arithmetic to select a range of lines for editing. For instance, a user can instruct **ed** to find the

Adding text:

a	Adds new lines
i	Inserts new lines
r	Reads the contents of a file

Modifying text:

d	Deletes lines
c	Replaces (changes) lines
m	Moves lines
t	Copies (duplicates) lines
j	Joins two lines to make one long line
k	Marks a line for later reference
s	Substitutes one piece of text for another

Printing text:

p	Prints lines on the terminal display
n	Prints lines, along with their line numbers
l	Prints lines, including nonprinting control characters

Miscellaneous:

h	Displays help messages on the terminal display
u	"Undoes" the effects of the last command
!	Executes a shell command from within the editor
w	Writes a copy of the text, including editing changes, into a text file
q	Terminates the editing session

*Table 10.2. Commonly Used **ed** Editing Commands*

word *contract* in a document and delete the next ten lines, all in a single editing command.

The pattern-matching capabilities available for selecting lines to edit are quite comprehensive. Typical pattern searches may include the following:

- Exact matching of a string of characters
- Wild-card matching of one or more characters
- Matching of text only at the beginning or end of a line

The **ed** utility can be instructed to search either forward or backward through the text to find matching lines. Figure 10.2 illustrates a short editing session.

This utility is limited to editing text files that fit in their entirety into the main memory editing buffer. Longer documents may be broken into sections or chapters for editing, with each section stored in its own text file. File-processing utilities can be used to split apart a large

```
$ ed                          # invoke ed
r results                     # read results into buffer
360                           # ed indicates file length
4,5p                          # print lines 4 and 5
Harris      newyork   east        0491207    19425
Harris      newyork   east        0421007    30000
4,5s/Harris/Greene/       # substitute text
4,5p                          # print lines 4 and 5 again
Greene      newyork   east        0491207    19425
Greene      newyork   east        0421007    30000
w                             # write the modified text to disk
360                           # file length hasn't changed
q                             # exit the editing session
$
```

*Fig. 10.2. A sample **ed** editing session.*

file for editing and then reassemble it for printing. If an extremely large file must be edited directly, the XENIX stream editor, **sed**, may be used. This utility was described in Chapter 9.

Screen-Oriented Editing with vi

The **vi** (**vi**sual editor) utility is an interactive, screen-oriented editor that has become quite popular among XENIX users. Like the **ed** editor, **vi** copies the contents of a text file into a buffer in main memory for editing. However, **vi** uses the terminal display as a "window" into the buffer, showing approximately twenty lines of text on the display at all times. On command, the window can be moved up and down through the buffer so that the user can examine the entire contents of the buffer. Figure 10.3 shows how the terminal display and editing buffer interact when **vi** is used.

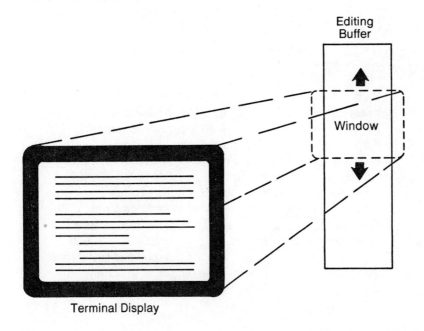

Fig. 10.3. Editing with vi.

To edit text, the user simply moves the cursor about the display, using single-character commands. These commands also move the cursor forward and backward through the text—a character, a word, a sentence, or a line at a time. Other editing commands are used to insert, modify, and delete text. The command specifies whether editing is to be performed on a character, a word, or a line. The results of each editing command are immediately reflected on the terminal display.

In addition to editing text directly on the terminal display, **vi** includes a set of editing commands similar to those available with the **ed** utility. These **vi** commands make mass changes to an entire document or to ranges of lines within the document. Again, **vi** immediately updates the displayed text to reflect each editing command.

Developed at Berkeley, the **vi** editor has become a popular addition to the various versions of UNIX. The utility is included as a standard part of the XENIX system.

Text Formatting with nroff

The **nroff** (**new runoff**) utility formats the contents of a text file for printing. The utility accepts a text file as input and produces a formatted document, ready for printing, as its output file. The input file contains text in free format, which can be edited by a user without regard to its final appearance on the printed page. The output file contains formatted text, complete with paragraph indentations, page headings, centered titles, and so on.

A user controls document formatting with formatting commands that are included with the text in the input file. The **nroff** utility interprets as commands, rather than text, any lines that begin with a period in column one. For example, the command **.bp** instructs **nroff** to begin a new page when formatting the document. Table 10.3 lists some commonly used **nroff** commands.

One of the most often used **nroff** functions is text justification. The **nroff** utility arranges text within user-specified margins on the page. At the user's option, **nroff** can left-justify or right-justify text, or both. Other capabilities of **nroff** include the following:

.ad l	Specifies left justification
.ad r	Specifies right justification
.ad c	Specifies center justification
.ad b	Specifies left and right justification
.bp	Starts a new page
.br	Breaks text, beginning a new line
.ce	Centers text
.de	Defines a text-processing macro
.fi	Turns on text filling
.hw	Specifies word hyphenation
.hy	Turns on hyphenation
.in	Indents a paragraph
.ll	Sets line length
.ls	Sets line spacing
.na	Turns off text adjusting (justification)
.ne	Keeps text together on a single page
.nf	Turns off text filling
.nh	Turns off hyphenation
.pl	Sets page length
.po	Sets page offset
.pn	Sets page number
.sp	Produces blank lines
.ti	Indents a single line
.tl	Specifies a three-part title
.ul	Underlines text
.wh	Sets traps for macro processing

*Table 10.3. Common **nroff** Formatting Commands*

- Automatic page header/footer printing
- Automatic footnoting
- Automatic section numbering
- Multicolumn printing
- Line spacing and line length control
- Line indentation

Figure 10.4 shows a simple text file with embedded formatting commands and the resulting output when the file is processed by **nroff.**

Input text file:

```
.ll 50                          # set line length of 50
.ce 2                           # center next 2 lines
.cu 2                           # underline next 2 lines
Sales Analysis by Region
November, 1983
.sp 2                           # skip 2 lines
.ti 5                           # indent next line 5 spaces
November proved to be an excellent month,
with all regions once again turning in good
sales performances.
Special recognition is due to
John Davis
in the
Boston
office, who led the sales force in orders.
```

Formatted output file:

```
              Sales Analysis by Region
                November, 1983


       November proved to be an excellent month,
with all regions once again turning in good sales
performances. Special recognition is due to John
Davis in the Boston office, who led the sales force
in orders.
```

*Fig. 10.4. An **nroff** formatting example.*

*Phototypesetting with **troff***

Troff (typesetter runoff) offers the same basic set of formatting functions as **nroff** but with expanded capabilities to support high-resolution printing devices. These devices can print text in different fonts, including roman, italic, and bold characters; and greek and special math characters. The **troff** utility also gives the user control over type size and supports proportional spaced printing.

Text-Formatting Macros

The **nroff** and **troff** utilities provide precise control over the appearance of printed output. Using these utilities directly is a tedious operation, however, because several commands are required to specify simple functions that are used again and again, such as "start a new paragraph by skipping a line and indenting 5 spaces."

For a higher level of support for common document processing, several macro packages have been developed. These packages offer predefined formatting commands. In place of several **nroff** commands, the macro packages provide single commands for functions like page numbering, setting up a table of contents, formatting a memo, forming the salutation and closing of a business letter, and so on. Most users use **nroff** and **troff** through these macro packages instead of using the utilities directly.

Specialized Text Formatting

Documents produced with the text-processing utilities will often include tabular data. The **tbl** (**table** formatter) utility formats tabular data of up to 35 columns for printing by the **nroff** or **troff** formatters. This utility is a filter, used as a preprocessor for these utilities. As is true for **nroff** and **troff**, the user controls the **tbl** utility through formatting commands embedded in the text file.

The printed appearance of a table within a document can be controlled through **tbl** commands that perform the following tasks:

- Left- or center-justify the table in the document
- Enclose the table in a box or double box
- Expand the table to fill the width of a text line
- Enclose each item of the table in a box

Detailed control over the format of each column in the table is also available through formatting commands that specify the following:

- Type font
- Type size
- Column width
- Left/right/center/numeric justification
- Text spanning across several columns

Figure 10.5 shows a file with **tbl** commands, along with the resulting output.

Another utility, **eqn** (**eq**uation formatter) is used to format mathematical equations that include special symbols.

Writing Aids

XENIX not only provides assistance in text editing and formatting, but also can help the user to improve writing style and correctness. The following four XENIX utilities constitute a family of writing aids to help an author write more effectively:

- The **spell** utility locates spelling errors in a document. Potential spelling or typographical errors are listed as output. The utility is based on a spelling dictionary, and auxiliary dictionaries can be used for specialized vocabularies.
- The **style** utility reports on the readability of a document by statistically analyzing the length and structure of its sentences. For example, several different "readability indexes" can be computed, along with lists of passive sentences.
- The **diction** utility finds sentences in a document that contain awkward or redundant phrases. The utility uses a data base containing common examples of bad or wordy diction.
- The **explain** utility suggests alternatives to the phrases identified by **diction**.

Calculation Tools

The **dc** (**d**esktop **c**alculator) utility is a general-purpose calculating tool. The utility simulates a handheld calculator that uses *reverse polish* notation, as in those marketed by Hewlett-Packard. This kind of calculator stores calculation results on a "push-down stack,"

Input text file:

```
.TS                    # start table
allbox;                # enclose each table element in a box
c s s s s              # center first line and span all columns
c c c c c              # center each column in second line
l l l l n              # left and numeric justifications
Sales Results
Salesman  Office    Region    Customer      Amount

Jones     boston    east      0221349       60000
Jones     boston    east      0213412       57995
Davis     boston    east      0210497        4650
Harris    newyork   east      0491207       19425
Harris    newyork   east      0421007       30000
Andrews   phila     east      0412095        2950
.TE                    # end of table
```

Formatted output file:

Sales Results				
Salesman	Office	Region	Customer	Amount
Jones	boston	east	0221349	60000
Jones	boston	east	0213412	57005
Davis	boston	east	0210497	4650
Harris	newyork	east	0491207	19425
Harris	newyork	east	0421007	30000
Andrews	phila	east	0412095	2950

*Fig. 10.5. A **tbl** formatting example.*

which is particularly useful for chain calculations in which the result of one calculation step is used in subsequent steps. The **dc** calculator offers over one hundred memory registers to store intermediate calculation results for later use. Table 10.4 lists the operations available with **dc**.

Arithmetic operations:

+	Addition
-	Subtraction
*	Multiplication
/	Division
%	Remainder (after division)
^	Exponentiation (x to the power y)
v	Square root

Commands:

p	Prints the top of stack
s	Stores the top of stack in a memory register
l	Recalls a memory register onto the top of stack
f	Prints the contents of the stack and registers
d	Duplicates the value on the top of stack
c	Clears the stack

Table 10.4. Desktop Calculator Features

The **dc** utility automatically handles arbitrarily large or small numbers in its calculations, with no loss of accuracy. Unlike typical desktop calculators, which store numbers internally to an accuracy of 8 or 14 digits, **dc** automatically adjusts its internal storage methods to store each number as precisely as possible. This feature can be very important when calculating, for example, with interest rates computed to thousandths of a percent in combination with account balances of millions of dollars. Normally, **dc** accepts input and displays its results in decimal (base 10) notation. For convenience to programmers, however, **dc** can also work in octal (base 8) and hexadecimal (base 16) notation. Figure 10.6 shows a short **dc** calculation to compute the circumference and area of a circle.

The **dc** calculator is also programmable. A sequence of keystrokes (single-character commands, entered numbers, etc.) can be stored in one of the calculator's memory registers and later executed au-

Given a circle, what is its circumference and area?

```
$ dc         # shell command invokes the desk calculator
             program
3.1416       # enter the value of pi
sA           # store it in register A for later recall
7.5          # enter the radius
sB           # store it in register B for later recall
lB           # recall radius from register B
2            # enter the number 2
*            # multiply 2 x radius to get diameter
lA           # recall pi
*            # multiply pi x diameter to get circumference
p            # print result
47.191
lB           # recall radius from register B
d            # duplicate top of stack
*            # multiply to get radius squared
lA           # recall pi
*            # multiply to get area
p            # print the result
176.715
```

Fig. 10.6. A sample **dc** *calculation.*

tomatically with a single command. Results of calculations can also be tested within a program, to execute different instructions based on these results. This feature is especially useful when the same calculation must be repeated over and over again on different data.

A companion utility, **bc**, offers even more programmability. This utility adds programming language constructs to the basic calculation features of **dc**. The **bc** utility is comparable in programming power to the simpler versions of the BASIC language. The utility's programming language constructs include the following:

- Variables with single-character names
- Begin/end blocks
- Conditional testing (**if...then**)
- Looping (**while...**)

- Iteration (**for...**)
- Multiline functions

Another XENIX utility offers specialized calculation support. The **units** utility performs units conversion for scientific and engineering calculations, such as centimeters-to-inches and pounds-to-kilograms calculations.

The Mail Facility

The **mail** utility provides the ability to send and receive electronic mail among users of a XENIX system. The **mail** facility offers a simple, effective, and often-used communication tool. Using the XENIX communications facilities, the mail facility can send mail to users of other XENIX or UNIX systems over the public telephone network.

Users send mail to other users on the same XENIX system by user name. Mail can also be sent to users on other XENIX systems by giving both the name of the system and the user's name on that system. A configuration file maintained by the system administrator is used to locate the remote system. An exclamation point is used to indicate a remote system name. The name

boston!joe

refers to the user named **joe** on the **boston** system.

The mail facility can even route mail through one or more intermediate systems to its final destination. The name

boston!newyork!henry

refers to the user **henry** on the **newyork** system, which is reached by sending mail through the **boston** system.

For short messages the **mail** utility can be used to enter interactively the text of the message. Input text is taken from the terminal, as in the following example:

```
$ mail joe sam
Subject: Budgets
Did you receive the report from accounting last week?
Our departments were 10% over budget, and we need to
discuss the situation. Please call me today. -- George
Cc: bob
(end of message)
$ ▋
```

Longer messages can be prepared with one of the XENIX text editors and stored in a text file. Redirecting the mail command's standard input to this file will transmit the message. For instance, the command

```
$ mail joe sam < memo
$ ▋
```

will send as mail the text file **memo** to users **joe** and **sam**.

Each user of the system has a separate *mailbox* to receive incoming mail. The **mail** utility is also used to examine the mailbox and dispose of incoming mail. A list of the messages in the mailbox is presented on the screen, showing the message number, sender, date, and subject. To dispose of messages, the user can select from numerous options, including the following:

- View a message on the display screen
- Delete a message
- Reply to a message with a new message
- Forward a message to another user
- Save the message in the user's mailbox or a file
- Edit a message with one of the XENIX text editors
- Print a message on the system printer
- List the size of each message

As with many XENIX utilities, the user may also execute a shell command from within the **mail** facility. This ability allows the user to take immediate action on incoming mail, for example, by printing a report or starting a program.

The **mail** facility also allows a user to define an *alias*, which is a single name representing an entire list of users. This capability is convenient for maintaining distribution lists for use with **mail**.

Calendar and Reminder Services

A pair of XENIX utilities provides an on-line calendar and a reminder service for office support. The **cal** utility prints a calendar for any month or year requested by the user, offering a convenient way to look up future and past dates without leaving the terminal. The **cal** operation is very straightforward, as illustrated here:

```
$ cal 11 1983
November 1983
     S    M   Tu    W   Th    F    S
               1    2    3    4    5
     6    7    8    9   10   11   12
    13   14   15   16   17   18   19
    20   21   22   23   24   25   26
    27   28   29   30

$ █
```

The **calendar** utility implements a simple reminder service for XENIX users. It scans a *calendar file* and displays lines that contain either today's date or tomorrow's date. The utility recognizes common methods of representing dates. (For example, it finds 10/14, Oct. 14, and October 14.)

In typical XENIX style the **calendar** utility offers users flexibility in formatting their reminder messages. Appointments are stored in free form in the calendar file, with one appointment per line. As long as the appointment date appears somewhere in the line, the **calendar** utility will locate it successfully. All other details (such as information stored about each appointment, order of fields on the line, and length of the line) are left to the user's discretion. Thus, each user on the system can have a personal method for organizing a calendar and still use one common utility program to receive reminders.

The Message Facility

In usual daily operation a XENIX system will have many users at terminals located throughout an organization. Some users may even use the system remotely over telephone lines. The message facility offers a quick and easy service for sending short messages between users who are logged in.

The **write** utility sends a message to another user. After giving the name of the user for whom the message is destined, the utility accepts input from the sender, line by line. To send a short message to user **george**, the user named **sam** types the following:

```
$ write george
I need to see you before lunch today to discuss
the McPherson deal. How about 11:30? -- sam
$ █
```

The message is terminated by typing the *end-of-file* character (**Control-D**) and is displayed by the **write** utility on the receiving user's terminal, line by line, as the sender types the message. An introductory line identifies the source of the message:

```
Message from sam tty10...
I need to see you before lunch today to discuss
the McPherson deal. How about 11:30? -- sam
(end of message)
```

At times, receiving unsolicited messages from another user can be a great inconvenience. For example, if a user is in the middle of editing a carefully formatted text document when a message arrives, the message will appear on the screen in the midst of the document text, disturbing its appearance. The XENIX system allows a user to control receipt of messages from other users with the **mesg** utility. The command

```
$ mesg n
$ █
```

prevents further receipt of messages until the user decides to accept them once again, with the following command:

```
$ mesg y
$ ▮
```

Another utility, **wall** (**w**rite to **all** users), is used by the system administrator to broadcast a message to all users who are currently
logged onto the system. This utility is normally used to warn users
of impending system shutdowns and similar events.

11
Software Development

The UNIX system has always enjoyed an excellent reputation as a software development tool. In fact, many computer science experts claim that UNIX, along with the C programming language, is the best environment available for developing complex systems and applications software products. Most of the leading suppliers of microcomputer software—including Digital Research, MicroPro, and others—develop software in C under UNIX. The UNIX/C combination is even popular for developing software that will run on mainframe systems and on microcomputers that do not themselves run UNIX. In this "cross-development" environment, programmers use UNIX to develop software for applications as diverse as computer games, robotics, and electronic test equipment. XENIX specifically includes cross-development tools to support the development of MS-DOS-based applications under XENIX.

Providing an excellent environment for serious software development was one of the goals of the UNIX system from the very beginning. Software development was the major UNIX application within Bell Labs, where UNIX was created. UNIX also plays a major role in computer science education in colleges and universities, where UNIX's popularity grew in the 1970s. Over 80 percent of the colleges that award computer science degrees are AT&T licensees for the UNIX system. It is difficult for a student to earn a degree in computer science today without substantial exposure to UNIX and its concepts. In fact, the universities have been turning out a steady stream of UNIX enthusiasts, who have formed the core of the UNIX popularity boom of the last few years. The availability of XENIX on low-cost microcomputer systems has contributed to this boom.

This chapter describes the XENIX system's programming tools and how they work together to make XENIX a superior environment for serious software development.

The XENIX Software Development Environment

The XENIX features that support software development include most of the capabilities described previously in this book. The hierarchical XENIX file system, for example, offers a natural way to organize the hundreds of individual files required to support a programming team. Program source code, test files, development tools, and object programs can all be organized to support effective individual work by each programmer, yet they offer sharing of common modules and tools. Similarly, programmers use the XENIX file-processing and text-processing utilities extensively to create, edit, and test programs, and to connect them together into complete applications systems.

The following features of the XENIX system are specifically targeted to support effective software development by a team of programmers:

- *The C programming language.* XENIX and C are intimately connected, with many XENIX facilities particularly well suited to C programming. C offers an excellent compromise between demands for a high-level language that makes a programmer efficient and a low-level language that gives the programmer direct access to hardware features.

- *The software tools approach.* The structure of XENIX encourages programmers to develop tools that assist in the development process. Spending the time to develop a specialized software tool that speeds subsequent development is a time-honored practice in UNIX software development. The XENIX pipe structure also allows programmers to create these new tools by connecting existing tools in new ways.
- *The Source Code Control System (SCCS).* SCCS helps to manage and coordinate software development by a team of programmers working on interrelated projects. With SCCS, changes to a large pool of software source code can be carefully managed and tracked, keeping team software development coordinated and under control.
- *Libraries.* XENIX maintains system-defined and user-defined libraries of software routines that perform commonly needed application functions. By including these routines into new programs, programmers can cut development time and ensure consistency across a wide body of software.
- *Communications tools.* XENIX systems are often used as development tools for software that will execute on other, non-XENIX systems. XENIX communications utilities, described in Chapter 12, allow software developed on a XENIX system to be effectively downloaded to other systems for testing and execution.

The C Programming Language

The histories of the UNIX system and the C programming language are closely linked, and a special relationship exists between the operating system and the programming language. XENIX itself is almost exclusively written in C. Thus, XENIX exists only on systems that have C compilers. Several general-purpose XENIX utilities, such as **awk** and **bc**, accept commands that are modeled on C programming language features. Other utilities, such as **lint**, are specifically targeted to support software development in C.

The primary reason for the popularity of the C programming language is its excellent compromise between two opposite but important demands commonly placed on programming languages. *Efficiency for programmers* is needed to maximize programmer effectiveness when new software is developed. *Efficiency for computers* is needed in the resulting software so that it performs well when it is executed.

Many studies have shown that a programmer tends to produce the same number of lines of debugged program text, regardless of the programming language being used. Higher-level programming languages are therefore preferred for software development. Because each line in a higher-level programming language can express a more complex operation than a line in a lower-level language, applications programs written in higher-level languages are shorter and take less time to develop. These programs are also easier to understand and debug.

Higher-level languages, however, can be wasteful and produce inefficient programs. Because the programmer is far removed from the details of the computer's hardware features, the programs produced by a higher-level language cannot make maximum use of these features in the computer instructions that they produce. It is not unusual for a higher-level language to produce a program that is three or even five times as large as a program that is custom written in a low-level assembly language by an expert programmer. The performance of the resulting programs can also differ by as much as five to one.

The C language offers programmers an ideal blend of high-level features and low-level efficiency for many programming tasks:

- C is a block-structured programming language that encourages conceptual, top-down programming techniques. Programs are built from functions, which themselves rest on lower-level functions. Altogether they yield a clear modular structure.
- C gives programmers low-level control over machine features for developing system software or for performance tuning an application. For example, a programmer can designate variables to be kept in high-performance registers and directly manipulate bit-level data without resorting to assembly language.

- C is flexible, with a variety of data types, a rich set of operators, and a small but capable set of programming commands.
- C is a very compact core language, with an extensive library of routines supporting common functions. Users can effectively extend the language by creating their own libraries of user-defined functions.

One of the most important features of C is its portability. Though C offers programmers the power of bit-level data manipulation, the language itself is independent of the arrangement of stacks, registers, and other features of a particular processor. C compilers are available for many systems, from 8-bit microprocessors to mainframes and supercomputers.

C programs are structured as a collection of functions. Each function is a self-contained module with its own arguments, a return value, and local storage and processing operations. Functions call on other, lower-level functions to perform their work. This structure encourages modular, top-down programming and lends itself naturally to software development by a team of programmers working independently.

Data Types

C supports a variety of data types, for representing naturally different types of data. In addition to the integer, character, and floating-point data types that are typical of all languages, C offers compound data types as well. *Arrays* of data provide an effective way to organize tables and lists. *Structures* are used to group together related data items into a single entity. For example, the individual pieces of data available for a customer— name, address, account balance, and so forth—can be combined into a structure and manipulated individually or as a unit in C. *Pointers* are used to identify the location of stored data and to form relationships among data elements. Using these data types, programmers can organize data in the way that is most natural for the application, instead of programming the application to fit a data organization dictated by the language.

Storage Classes

C offers the following types of data storage for data that is used in separate modules of a program:

- *Automatic* variables store data that is used only within a function. These variables are initialized each time the function is called and usually take up main memory space only when the function itself is executing.
- *Static* variables also contain private data that is used only within a function. But unlike automatic variables, static variables retain their previous values each time a function is called. A static variable is used, for example, to hold a count of how many times a function has been called.
- *External* variables contain data that is defined outside a function but which may be accessed and modified from within the function.
- *Register* variables give programmers a tool for performance tuning their programs. They are identified to the C compiler as variables that are frequently used and are therefore good candidates for storing in a computer's high-speed register hardware.

Because C is a portable language, there is no guarantee that register variables will, in fact, be stored in high-performance memory locations. However, the register storage class provides a hardware-independent method for identifying this kind of data in the language.

Operators

The C language includes a rich assortment of operators to compute, manipulate, and compare data. The normal arithmetic operations are augmented with bit-level operators that perform logical operations and bit-level tests and that shift data. Auto-incrementing and auto-decrementing operations are also supported, offering programmers a natural way to process lists, arrays, and counts. Assignment operations are very flexible, with assignment operators combining arithmetic, logical, and auto-incrementing operations and value assignment in a single operation. The large assortment of operators available makes C programs more difficult to read for the novice but provides the experienced programmer with a compact, efficient way to express required computations.

Table 11.1 summarizes the main structures of the C programming language.

Data types:

    Pointer
    Structure (composite data type)

Storage classes:

    Automatic
    Static
    External
    Register

Unary operations:

    Negation
    Complement
    Logical negation
    Indirection
    Pointer
    Pre- and post-increment
    Pre- and post-decrement

Binary operations:

    Addition
    Subtraction
    Multiplication
    Division
    Remainder
    Bit-shifting (right/left)
    Bit-by-bit AND, OR, Exclusive OR

Table 11.1. (Continued on next page)

Relational tests:

>Equal
>Not equal
>Greater than
>Greater than or equal
>Less than
>Less than or equal

Functions:

>Return a single typed value
>Call-by-value arguments (except for arrays)

Statement types:

>Simple statement
>Block ({...})
>Conditional (**if...**, **if...else...**)
>Looping (**while...**, **do...while...**)
>Iteration (**for...**)
>Selection (**switch...**)
>Branching (**goto...**)

Compiler directives:

>Symbolic constant definition
>Inclusion of source text from a library
>Conditional compilation

Table 11.1. C Programming Language Features

Libraries

Libraries extend the power of the XENIX programming languages. A *library* is a collection of preprogrammed functions that perform specific, commonly needed tasks. These functions may be referenced in a program, and they are automatically linked into the program when it is prepared for execution. With these functions, programmers can tap the wealth of software already developed for the XENIX system and avoid duplication of effort. Functions in the library are called within a program just as if they had been written by the programmer.

The XENIX system has two standard libraries. To support other functions, users can expand these libraries or add their own libraries. For example, most data base management software packages include a library of functions for data base access from C programs. When this library is installed on the system, the functions are called by programs that access the data base.

The *C library*, supplied with the C language, is a collection of functions that extend C's capabilities. Over one hundred functions in this library give programmers convenient routines to perform the following:

- File input/output and status checking
- String manipulation, such as comparison and searching
- Character processing and testing for digits, uppercase/lowercase, etc.
- Date and time operations
- Numerical conversion from integers to floating point, etc.
- Encryption
- Access to the system's group and password files
- Processing of command options and shell variables
- Table searching for hash tables, binary trees, and lists
- Memory allocation and de-allocation
- Random number generation
- Mathematical functions, such as absolute value, trigonometric, and power functions

The *curses library* is a collection of screen input/output functions. These functions were described in Chapter 8.

Checking C Program Portability

The **lint** utility checks the syntax of C language programs. This utility helps programmers ensure that their C programs are transportable to other computer systems. The C programming language, because of its low-level operations, can be used to create programs that are hardware dependent. For example, a programmer may make assumptions about the internal format of a certain data type. These assumptions may be valid on one system but not others. The **lint** utility checks a C program using stricter rules than the C compiler and reports on program statements that may cause portability problems. The utility also performs other consistency checks on programs, such as verifying that variables are initialized before they are used, and locating statements that cannot be reached during program execution.

Other Program Development Tools

The XENIX system includes a number of other utilities that aid in the program development process. Table 11.2 lists a few of these utilities. Two of the most complex utilities in the UNIX system, **yacc** and **lex**, fall into this category. Both are tools originally designed to help programmers develop systems-level software, but these tools may also be used in the development of command-oriented applications programs.

The **lex** (**lex**ical analyzer) utility is used for command language processing. Many useful programs are command driven, requiring that programmers develop software routines to accept a line of text from the user and interpret it as a command with options and arguments. The **lex** utility builds this software automatically. The programmer gives **lex** a set of rules describing the acceptable commands, and **lex** produces routines that perform the lexical analysis of command lines, breaking them into their component pieces.

A companion utility, **yacc** (**y**et **a**nother **c**ompiler **c**ompiler), picks up where **lex** leaves off. Like **lex**, **yacc** produces a set of software routines as its output. The programmer gives **yacc** a set of rules describing the command language and the actions to take when each command or command option is recognized. Then **yacc** translates these specifications into software routines that implement the command language described by the user. The **yacc** and **lex** utilities can be used together to reduce greatly the development time for producing command-driven software products, such as compilers and editors.

In addition to the software development tools that are included with XENIX, a selection of other languages has been developed by Microsoft and other third-party software suppliers.

cc	Compiles and links C programs
as	Assembles Intel 8088/8086 assembly language programs
lint	Checks the syntax of C programs
cb	Formats a C program with indentation and spacing
cref	Generates a C program cross-reference listing
adb	Aids in object code debugging
ld	Links program modules into an object file
od	Generates an octal dump
hd	Generates a hexadecimal dump
strings	Searches for text strings in an object file
nm	Prints the symbol table from an object program file
size	Displays the size of object program files
hdr	Displays linkage information from an object program file
lex	Generates programs to perform lexical analysis
yacc	Aids in development of compilers, interpreters, and complex command-driven programs
lorder	Lists the external identifiers in each object file in a library or archive
strip	Strips symbol table information from an object file

Table 11.2. (Continued on next page)

ar	Maintains archives and libraries
m4	Performs macro preprocessing
make	Determines the sequence of steps required to recompile a complex program comprised of many different modules, some of which have been updated

Table 11.2. Program Development Utilities

The Source Code Control System

The XENIX *Source Code Control System* (SCCS) is a collection of utilities designed to assist the management of large-scale software development projects. Although originally developed to manage files containing program source code, SCCS can be applied equally as well to managing almost any collection of text files. SCCS organizes changes to the files into a series of versions and revisions of the text, allowing users to access the precise version that they need.

SCCS can also restrict changes to the files it manages, permitting only a specific list of users to modify each file. These utilities track each change to a file, recording its purpose, the name of the user who made the change, and the time of the modification. SCCS stores and retrieves different versions of each file, allowing recovery from errors and "roll back" to earlier versions. Most important, SCCS prevents several users from trying to change the same version of a file at the same time.

SCCS operation is easy to understand by comparing it to a public library. The individual files under SCCS control correspond to the books in the library, with SCCS in the librarian's role. To work on any of the files, a user "checks out" the file, and SCCS notes which file was withdrawn, when, and by whom. A file can be withdrawn for examination only, or it can be withdrawn with the intention to revise it. Once withdrawn, a file can be edited and processed, using the normal XENIX text-processing tools. If the file contains program source code, it will likely be compiled, tested, and perhaps recompiled many times over, with intermediate editing sessions.

Normally, SCCS will only allow one user at a time to withdraw any given version of an SCCS file for modification. This limitation prevents multiple users from making conflicting changes to the file. When the user is satisfied with the changes made, the file is returned. SCCS stores the revisions as a new version of the file, along with a user-supplied comment as to why the revisions were made. Changes can be made only to files that were withdrawn for modification.

Figure 11.1 illustrates the role of SCCS in text management. The **get** and **delta** utilities withdraw files from the SCCS pool and introduce altered files back into the pool, respectively.

SCCS Version Control

SCCS stores each file under its control as an "original" file, plus a sequence of updates to the file, called *deltas*, which contain only the modifications made to the file. By organizing its files in this way, SCCS maintains many different versions of each file, using much less disk space than would be required to store each version in its entirety. SCCS numbers the various versions of a file, using a four-level numbering scheme, shown in figure 11.2. By convention, the *release number* is used to identify major new versions of a text file. Normally, changes are identified by incrementing the *level number*, indicating a new revision within the same release. The original version of each SCCS text file is identified as version 1.1, the next version is version 1.2, and so on.

At times, several different authors will make different modifications to the same version of a text file. SCCS accommodates these modifications by creating a *branch* version of the text, using the remaining two levels of its four-level numbering scheme. Branching can occur over and over again, as shown in figure 11.3. Note that three different current versions of the text have been developed from a common original text through different sets of modifications.

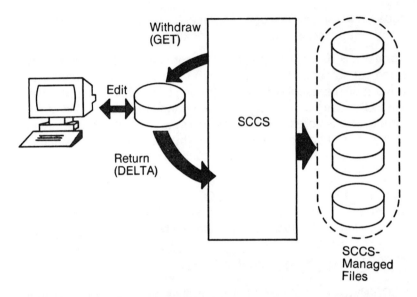

Fig. 11.1. Source Code Control System.

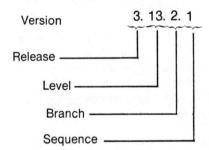

Fig. 11.2. SCCS version numbering.

SCCS Security

SCCS implements additional security features, beyond those of the XENIX file system, for tight control over file modification. For each

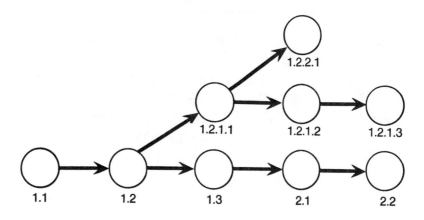

Fig. 11.3. SCCS versions with branching.

file managed by SCCS, the owner may specify a list of users and/or user groups who are allowed to create new versions of the file. The owner can also lock specific versions of an SCCS file against further modification. These versions can be withdrawn from SCCS for inspection but cannot be modified. A specific range of versions can also be specified as the only versions of a file that are available for updating.

SCCS Management Utilities

In addition to allowing users to withdraw and resubmit files under its control, SCCS includes a number of utility functions to aid in file management. Using SCCS utilities, the user can perform the following:

admin	Places a file under SCCS control and changes its description
get	Obtains a version of an SCCS file for examination or editing
delta	Creates a new version of an SCCS file, including new editing changes
prs	Prints parts of an SCCS file
rmdel	Removes a version of an SCCS file, which was created in error
cdc	Changes the comments associated with a version of an SCCS file
what	Searches SCCS files for identified comments embedded in the text
sccsdiff	Prints the differences between versions of SCCS files
comb	Combines stored versions of SCCS files, obliterating part of the file's history
val	Validates SCCS files to ensure that they have a specified version number
unget	Notifies SCCS that a version withdrawn for editing will not be edited
help	Explains usage of SCCS commands

Table 11.3. SCCS Utilities

- Show the differences between two versions of a file
- Print the contents of a text file, with each line showing the version number, indicating when it was most recently changed

- Automatically insert information, such as the date, current version number, and name of the file, when the file is printed
- Show the history of a version of an SCCS file, listing all the versions that logically precede it
- Remove the latest version of an SCCS file, reverting back to the previous version to recover from major errors

Execution Profiling

Programmers concerned with the performance of their programs can use the **time** command to obtain information about program execution times. The command

```
$ time report1
real      35.1
user       2.1
sys        0.1
$ ■
```

executes the **report1** program and displays the elapsed wall clock time during the program's execution, the CPU time spent executing the program, and the CPU time spent within the XENIX kernel on behalf of the program.

Programmers can also compile a program with a profiling option to identify the areas in the program where performance can be improved. When the program is executed, a disk file is automatically generated that records the execution flow of the program over a period of time. The **prof** utility is used to analyze this data and to determine where a program is spending the largest percentage of its execution time. These sections of the program then become prime candidates for performance improvement work.

MS-DOS Cross-Development Tools

XENIX includes a complete C language cross-development environment for MS-DOS. The cross-development tools allow program-

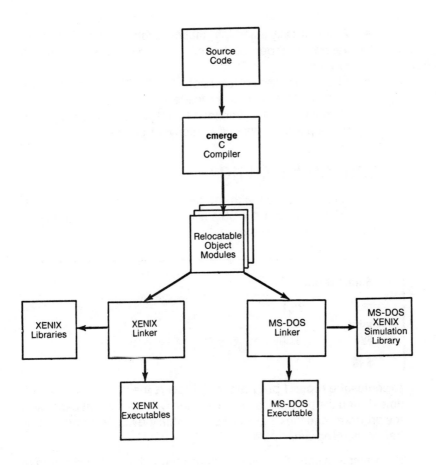

Fig. 11.4. Cross-development tools.

mers to use the excellent software development facilities of XENIX
to create applications intended for execution on PCs under
MS-DOS. Figure 11.4 graphically illustrates the cross-development
process.

The **cmerge** C language compiler supports this cross-development
environment. The compiler handles differences between XENIX and
MS-DOS, such as the word order within a long word. MS-DOS libraries included with the compiler simulate XENIX subroutines and

system calls under MS-DOS. Finally, relocatable object modules produced by the compiler for XENIX are identical in format with MS-DOS and portable to it.

Programs compiled with the **cmerge** compiler can be linked using either the XENIX or the DOS linker, for execution under either operating system. Using **cmerge** permits debugging under XENIX and eventual execution under MS-DOS without changes to source code.

12
Communications

XENIX includes several utilities that support system-to-system communications. Considering the origins of UNIX within AT&T, it is not surprising that many of these utilities support communications through the switched telephone network. In fact, electronic communications between UNIX systems has become a very popular alternative to mail services among experienced UNIX users in universities, research laboratories, and industrial companies around the world. An entire network of interconnected UNIX systems is available, and users can often be found routing messages through two or three intermediate machines to reach their ultimate destinations. XENIX includes most of the UNIX communications utilities and several additional utilities for XENIX-to-XENIX connections.

Communications Facilities

Utilities provided with the XENIX system support the following communications functions:

- *Remote login.* A user on one system can login to another system across a communications link. A user may execute commands on the remote system and perform other tasks as if the user were using the system directly.
- *File transfer.* A user on one system can transfer files to and from another system across a communications link.
- *Remote mail.* Mail can be sent to users on other systems through the XENIX mail facility, which was discussed in Chapter 10.

Remote Login to a XENIX System

The **cu** (**c**all **U**NIX) utility allows a user connected to a XENIX system to login temporarily to another XENIX or UNIX system. Figure 12.1 shows a typical **cu** connection. The local system may access the remote system directly over a dedicated communications line or indirectly over the public telephone network. If the local system is equipped with an automatic dialing modem, the user can specify a telephone number with the **cu** command, for automatic dialing of the remote system.

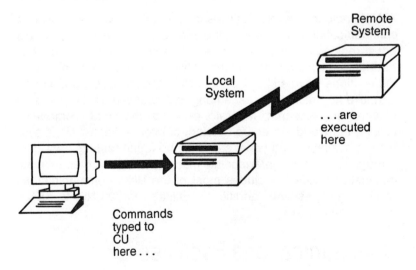

Remote
System

Local
System

... are
executed
here

Commands
typed to
CU
here ...

Fig. 12.1. Remote login with **cu***.*

Once the user is connected to the remote system, commands are
entered as if the user were directly logged on to the remote system.
The entered commands access the files and devices of the remote
system. The **cu** utility also supports other communications capabilities with the remote system, allowing a user to perform the following
tasks:

- Escape from the communications link to run a single com-
  mand on the local system
- Run a command on the remote system, capturing its out-
  put on the local system
- Run a command on the local system, sending its output to
  the remote system
- Copy a file from the local system to the remote system
- Copy a file from the remote system to the local system

The **cu** utility can even be used to communicate with non-UNIX systems and to assist in transfer of data files, conversion of programs,
and other communications functions.

Remote File Transfer

The **uucp** (**U**NIX-to-**U**NIX **c**opy) facility copies files from a XENIX
system to another XENIX or UNIX system across a communications
link. The facility is actually a family of utilities, as listed in table 12.1.

uucp	Copies files to and from a remote system
uusend	Copies files to a remote system through intermediate systems
uunow	Initiates a **uucp** connection
uulog	Prints information about file copy activity from a log file
uux	Executes commands on a remote system, routing input and output from other systems

*Table 12.1. The **uucp** Utilities*

This facility identifies a remote file by its path name on the remote system. The name of the remote system is prefixed to the path name and separated from it by an *exclamation point* (!). The **uucp** path name

finance!/joe/report

identifies the file named **/joe/report** on the system named **finance**. The **uucp** facility uses a configuration file, maintained by the system administrator, to determine how to access a remote system. Details of the communications network are thus hidden from ordinary users.

The **uucp** facility also supports file transfers forwarded through intermediate systems. For example, the **uucp** path name

chicago!finance!/joe/report

identifies the file **/joe/report** on the **finance** system, which is accessed by sending messages through the **chicago** system.

Using the **uucp** utilities, the user can track the progress of a file transfer and request notification by XENIX mail when the transfer is complete. A user on the remote system can also be notified. The **uucp** facility can copy files directly or copy them to a temporary spool directory, freeing the original copy of the file for further use.

The **uucp** utilities use a communications protocol that automatically detects data transmission errors. Each record transmitted includes a calculated error detection field, which is recalculated when the record is received. A discrepancy means that an error has occurred, causing retransmission of the record. This error detection technique ensures that most communications errors will be detected and automatically corrected.

The Micnet Package

The Micnet package is an alternative communications facility to **uucp**. Micnet simplifies the creation and maintenance of local communications networks that use direct RS-232 connections. Micnet supports most of the capabilities offered by **uucp** but is simpler to use. For example, **netutil** is an interactive utility that configures the network, defining system names, communications lines, and transmission speeds. Micnet also has an interface to the XENIX **mail** facility, allowing transparent routing of mail among the systems in a Micnet network. Table 12.2 lists the Micnet utilities.

netutil	Interactively defines the network configuration and supports other network administration tasks
remote	Executes commands on a remote system
rcp	Copies files to and from a remote system

Table 12.2. Micnet Utilities

13

The Future of XENIX

Predicting the future of XENIX and the overall UNIX market has become a favorite pastime among market researchers and the computer trade press. Most of the "experts" agree that the market for microcomputer systems based on UNIX/XENIX will explode over the next few years. But the experts are divided in their forecasts of which UNIX version will dominate, or whether any version of UNIX can achieve a level of success like that of MS-DOS. This chapter provides a discussion of the factors and trends that influence the future of XENIX.

The XENIX system today is at a critical juncture in its product life. XENIX currently has the largest installed base of any UNIX version. In particular, XENIX dominates the low end of the multiuser microcomputer market. This position represents an opportunity for even higher sales volumes as multiuser systems begin to sell through retail computer stores. Finally, IBM's endorsement of XENIX on the PC AT *could* be the factor that pushes XENIX "over the top," establishing it as the multiuser microcomputer operating system standard.

Powerful forces, however, are working to limit the success of XENIX. AT&T is spending millions of dollars to establish its own UNIX System V as a standard. And despite XENIX's success on the Intel processor family, XENIX has been relatively unsuccessful on higher-performance Motorola 68000-based systems. IBM also offers several alternative versions of UNIX, and the company's commitment to XENIX is unclear. Availability of XENIX applications software is dwarfed by the myriad of software packages available under MS-DOS. Finally, the steady incorporation of XENIX features into MS-DOS poses a competitive threat from networked PC configurations.

AT&T and UNIX System V

One of the largest forces in the market for UNIX/XENIX systems today is the massive promotional campaign mounted by AT&T in support of UNIX System V. The advertising theme "System V: Consider It Standard" has blanketed computer trade journals and general business publications. The marketing campaign has heightened awareness of UNIX in general and has stirred up controversy over the different versions of UNIX.

Behind the marketing hype, Microsoft's enhancements to UNIX make XENIX a superior alternative to System V as a commercial operating system. AT&T has recognized these deficiencies and has begun to address them in UNIX System V, with such features as semaphores and interprocess communication. But the implementation of these new features is incompatible with their XENIX counterparts. Thus, with each new release of System V, the competitive advantage of the XENIX enhancements can rapidly become a disadvantage. Microsoft chairman Bill Gates announced in June, 1984, that XENIX would evolve to become System V-compatible. Recognizing the market force represented by XENIX, AT&T announced in January, 1985, a cooperative relationship with Microsoft. Nonetheless, maintaining compatibility with AT&T's UNIX developments is probably the largest technical challenge facing Microsoft.

AT&T has also altered the UNIX licensing policy, changing key provisions and lowering the license fees for small UNIX-based systems.

The new policy eliminates most of the financial leverage on which Microsoft's XENIX marketing strategy was based. In the long term, the XENIX market position must clearly be based on brand identity and volume distribution, not on an AT&T pricing umbrella.

The "Generic" Micro Ports

The "generic" micro ports represent a key part of AT&T's strategy for System V. These micro ports greatly reduce the effort of porting UNIX to a new microcomputer system and may therefore act as a force for standardization of System V. AT&T publicly claims that the micro ports are not part of a competitive assault on UNIX software suppliers. Nonetheless, these firms (and Microsoft in particular) have the most to lose from this part of AT&T's System V plan.

The impact of the micro ports has been blunted by serious delivery delays. As of early 1985, only the Motorola port was complete and being shipped. Intel had subcontracted its port to Digital Research, and National Semiconductor and Zilog were still working on their ports. Moreover, the micro ports are based on the first release of System V, which AT&T has superseded with subsequent releases. If the micro ports continue to fall behind, hardware manufacturers will still have to rely on their own in-house development groups or turn to software companies such as Microsoft to stay competitive with AT&T.

Independent Standards Efforts

In addition to AT&T's promotion of UNIX System V, other groups are also attempting to influence UNIX system standardization. The /usr/group standard represents one such effort. The American National Standards Institute (ANSI) is also involved, through a committee charged with standardizing the C programming language. Standardization of C is perhaps even more critical than standardization of UNIX itself because the differences among various implementations of the language are substantial.

These independent standards complement the efforts of AT&T and other proprietary interests in the UNIX marketplace. As always, the *real* standards will be set through widespread market acceptance of a product rather than through pronouncements by standards bodies. The competitive moves of AT&T and IBM will have far more impact on the success or failure of XENIX than will any independent standards efforts.

Microcomputer Technology Trends

The major trends in microcomputer technology are accelerating the acceptance of UNIX and XENIX. Using present technology, a XENIX-based IBM PC AT system with a 16/32-bit microprocessor, 64K memory chips, and a 20M byte hard disk can be purchased for under $8,000 and expanded to support three users. An equivalent system, based on the minicomputer technology of the late 1970s, would then have cost in excess of $50,000. XENIX-based systems have now moved within reach of most small businesses and even fit within the discretionary budgets of some department managers in large companies.

The microcomputer technology trends will continue to improve the price/performance of microcomputer systems, making XENIX available even on personal computers. These trends include the following:

- Over the next two to three years, true 32-bit microprocessors promise to double and triple the processing power available on a single chip. These processors can address large amounts of memory, and they include on-chip support for memory protection and virtual memory. The number of components required to build a XENIX system, and hence its cost, will drop dramatically as a result of these developments. Sample quantities of these new microprocessors (such as the Intel 80386 and the Motorola 68020) are becoming available, and they will form the basis of most medium- and high-end microcomputer systems by 1986.
- Advances in memory technology will continue to lower the cost of microcomputer memory. RAMs of 256K quadruple the current capacity per memory chip, and 256K is already the minimum standard memory capacity for personal computers. Larger microcomputers will routinely feature

two or three megabytes of memory. The larger memory requirements of XENIX, when compared to other personal computer operating systems, will thus become less of a consideration.

- The continued development of 5 1/4-inch Winchester disks will allow capacities exceeding a hundred megabytes in drives costing only a few hundred dollars. Hard disks will become the norm rather than the exception on personal computers. XENIX is a disk-intensive operating system and is unsuited for floppy-based systems. The trend to high-capacity, lower-cost disks makes XENIX an attractive alternative to floppy-based operating systems.

- Local area network (LAN) technology is just beginning to make its impact on microcomputers and XENIX systems. XENIX-based microcomputer systems distributed throughout a facility and connected through a LAN will replace centralized minicomputer installations for office automation and data processing applications. As the developer of IBM's PC network software, Microsoft is in an excellent position to incorporate network support into XENIX.

MS-DOS and XENIX

The success of MS-DOS as a personal computer operating system has delayed the acceptance of XENIX. As a result, Microsoft has slowly incorporated the most popular features of XENIX into successive MS-DOS releases. Microsoft intends to evolve MS-DOS even further in this direction, with the goal of eventually making MS-DOS a compatible subset of XENIX. XENIX has thus become both a competitor to MS-DOS and a source of inspiration for its continuing development.

In the future, PC networks based on MS-DOS will compete directly with multiuser XENIX systems as solutions to departmental and small business computing needs. The PC network approach has tremendous emotional appeal in the retail channel, where such a network takes advantage of existing PC software and sales techniques. In addition, the installed base of PCs forms a lucrative target for add-on network sales.

The appeal of PC networks is balanced by the complexity of selling and supporting them. And while some single-user PC applications (such as spreadsheets and graphics) can be transparently moved to networks, others (such as data base managers) require rewriting for network environments. Furthermore, serious data processing applications, such as order processing or inventory control, are extremely difficult to coordinate in a network and much easier to implement on a multiuser system.

In many applications a combination of multiuser systems and PCs on a single network may offer the best solution. At this writing, neither IBM nor Microsoft has announced PC network support for XENIX. Such support, however, is a very likely future XENIX enhancement.

The XENIX Applications Software Gap

The availability of applications software is the pacing factor in the acceptance of any operating system. Applications software for XENIX has been slow to emerge because most software developers have turned their attention to the much larger installed base of MS-DOS-based systems. XENIX software packages have begun to appear in larger numbers over the last year, and several hundred packages are now available. In general, the functional capability of these packages is superior to their MS-DOS counterparts, but a single package with the catalyzing effect of a product like Lotus 1-2-3 has not yet appeared.

XENIX software packages are coming from the following main sources:

- *Minicomputer software conversion.* Several popular minicomputer accounting packages have been converted to run under XENIX. Developers are also converting their optimizing compilers and sophisticated data base systems for use on XENIX-based systems.
- *PC software conversion.* Conversion of MS-DOS-based software to XENIX has thus far amounted to little more than a trickle. The notable PC packages currently available include a multiuser version of dBASE II from Ashton-Tate and Microsoft's Multiplan spreadsheet.

- *New UNIX-based development.* Most XENIX applications software is being developed by small software firms who specialize in C language software. Sophisticated data base packages have been available for several years; office automation applications are just starting to emerge.

The pace of XENIX software development has quickened with the introduction of the PC AT. In addition, IBM is actively pursuing UNIX/XENIX-based software for its publishing operation, which should encourage even more software development.

XENIX in the Retail Computer Market

XENIX has already penetrated the retail computer market. Tandy was an early pioneer in retailing XENIX-based systems, and Altos Computers has established a presence in a few high-end retail chains. Availability of XENIX on the IBM PC AT is the latest and perhaps most significant step in bringing multiuser systems into the retail channel.

Historically, multiuser systems have been a poor fit for the retail channel. They are complex, and the selling effort requires an analysis of the customer's applications needs, as well as a great deal of post-sales hand-holding and support. Often these systems are used in critical applications, such as accounting or payroll, where a system failure has far more serious consequences than the loss of a spreadsheet or a word-processing document on a PC. Multiuser systems thus require more highly trained sales people, a concentrated sales effort, and extensive post-sale support.

Multiuser systems, however, have one overriding advantage for the computer retailer: high profits. Typical multiuser systems sell for several times the price of a PC; more important, these systems also experience less competitive price pressure from discount and mail order sales. High-end retailers can thus afford the extra effort that multiuser systems require, but only if the post-sales costs can be contained.

For many retailers XENIX on the PC AT will become an experiment in selling multiuser systems. The acceptance of XENIX as a mainstream retail computer product will depend on these early successes or failures. The PC network alternative complicates the issue because it presents the same two-edged sword of high profits and high support costs.

IBM's UNIX Strategy

No single factor has a larger potential impact on the success or failure of XENIX than IBM's strategy for UNIX-based systems. IBM is sending out mixed signals on what that strategy may be. The company currently offers a bewildering array of different UNIX versions on different hardware systems:

- PC/IX on the PC XT and PC AT personal computers
- XENIX on the PC AT personal computer
- XENIX on the System 9000 multiuser M68000 system
- CP/IX on the Series I minicomputer
- VM/IX on the 4300 mainframe series

These ports are derived from different AT&T UNIX versions and have been developed both in-house and by outside software companies. Many rumors are circulating of other UNIX activity within IBM, including a System V port and a UNIX look-alike. There are also rumors of new UNIX-based hardware offerings, including a multiuser microcomputer more powerful than the PC AT and capable of supporting up to a dozen users.

UNIX poses a serious problem for IBM. On the one hand, UNIX could provide a tremendous unifying force across the entire IBM product line, bringing compatibility to the company's diverse hardware offerings. On the other hand, UNIX is controlled by AT&T, IBM's largest potential competitor. The resulting IBM posture appears to be a defensive one. UNIX is offered on several different systems in response to customer pressure. But UNIX is a tactical product, not a strategic one emphasized in IBM marketing programs.

Other interpretations of IBM's actions are possible. The company may not, in fact, have a single, centralized UNIX strategy. A more sinister interpretation has IBM deliberately disrupting the UNIX promotion and standardization efforts of AT&T by proliferating incompatible versions.

Of all the UNIX versions offered by IBM, XENIX seems to have the best chance of becoming a strategic IBM product. The relationship between Microsoft and IBM appears very strong. Microsoft software will undoubtedly form the foundation of a networked PC product line that stretches from "laptop" machines to high-end supermicros. The role played by XENIX in that product line remains an open question. The answer to that question will have dramatic consequences for the future of XENIX, and of the entire UNIX marketplace.

Appendix A

XENIX System Calls

File and Device Input/Output

open	Open a file for input/output
close	Conclude input/output to a file
read	Read data from file
rdchk	Check whether there is data to be read
write	Write data to file
lseek	Move file pointer in file
locking	Lock a region of a file
ioctl	Device control operations
fcntl	File control operations
fstat	Get file status information
dup,dup2	Duplicate file descriptor
chdir	Change working directory
chroot	Change to a different root directory

File Creation, Status, and Security

creat	Create a new file
mknod	Create a directory or special file
link	Create a new link to a file

223

unlink	Remove a link to a file
access	Get file access permissions
chmod	Change file access permissions
chown	Change the owner of a file
chsize	Change the size of a file
utime	Change file access/modification times
stat	Get file status
umask	Set/get file creation mask
mount	Mount a file system
umount	Unmount a file system
ustat	Get file system statistics

Process Control

exec	Execute a new program
pause	Suspend process, awaiting a signal
alarm	Set process alarm clock
nap	Sleep for a short time
exit	Terminate process
fork	Start a child process
walt	Await termination of child process
kill	Terminate or send signal to a process
signal	Specify action in response to signal
nice	Change process priority

Process Status

getpid	Get process id number
getppid	Get parent process id number
setpgrp	Set process group id number
getpgrp	Get process group id number
setuid	Set user id number
getuid	Get user id number
setgid	Set group id number
getgid	Get group id number
geteuid	Get effective user id number
getegid	Get effective group id number
times	Get process execution time information
ulimit	Get and set process limits

sbrk,brk	Request additional main memory for a process
lock	Lock a process in main memory

Interprocess Communications and Shared Memory

pipe	Create a pipe
sdget	Attach a shared data segment
sdfree	Detach a shared data segment
sdenter	Request exclusive access to a shared data segment
sdleave	Relinquish exclusive access to a shared data segment
sdgetv	Get version number of a shared data segment
sdwaitv	Wait for change in version number of a shared data segment

Process Synchronization

creatsem	Create a semaphore
opensem	Open a semaphore
waitsem	Wait on a semaphore
nbwaitsem	Wait on a semaphore, without blocking
sigsem	Signal a semaphore

Miscellaneous

acct	Enable/disable accounting
profil	Enable/disable executing profiling
ptrace	Trace execution of child process
stime	Set time and date
time	Get time of day
ftime	Get system time
sync	Flush kernel file buffers
shutdn	Flush file buffers and halt system
uname	Get name of current XENIX system

Appendix B

Utilities in XENIX

acctcom	Prints process accounting files
accton	Turns accounting on/off
adb	Absolute debugger
admin	Creates and administers SCCS files
ar	Maintains portable archives
as	Assembler
asktime	Sets system date and time
assign	Grants exclusive access to a device
at	Runs a program at a specified time
awk	Pattern scanning and processing language
banner	Makes banners
basename	Outputs the file name from a path name
bc	Desktop calculator with programming constructs
bdiff	Compares two large files
bfs	Scans big files
cal	Outputs a calendar
calendar	Appointment scheduler
cat	Concatenates and prints files
cb	Formats C programs
cc	C language compiler

cd	Changes the current working directory
cdc	Changes comments for an SCCS delta
chgrp	Changes group ownership of a file
chmod	Changes file access permissions
chown	Changes ownership of a file
cmp	Compares two files
col	Filters reverse line feeds
comb	Combines SCCS deltas
comm	Selects or rejects lines common to two sorted files
copy	Copies groups of files
cp	Copies files
cpio	Copies file archives
cpp	C language preprocessor
cref	Generates a C program cross reference
cron	Launches programs at specified times
crypt	Encodes and decodes files
csh	C shell
csplit	Splits files based on pattern matching
ctags	Creates a tags file from C source code
cu	Calls another UNIX/XENIX system
cut	Selects columns from a tabular file
cw	Prepares constant-width text for troff
date	Sets and prints the date
dc	Desktop calculator
dd	Performs file transformations
deassign	Relinquishes exclusive access to a device
delta	Makes a change to an SCCS file
deroff	Removes formatting commands from a file
df	Displays information about free disk space
diction	Finds awkward phrases in text
diff	Compares two files
diff3	Compares three files
diffmk	Marks the differences between files
dircmp	Compares directories
dirname	Outputs the path from a path name
disable	Disables spooling on a printer
doscat	Concatenates files on a PC DOS floppy disk
doscp	Copies files to/from a PC DOS floppy disk
dosdir	Lists the directory of a PC DOS floppy disk

dosmkdir	Creates a directory on a PC DOS floppy disk
dosrm	Deletes files from a PC DOS floppy disk
dosrmdir	Deletes directories from a PC DOS floppy disk
dtype	Prints disk type (XENIX, PC DOS, tar, etc.)
du	Summarizes disk usage
dump	Dumps selected parts of an object file
dumpdir	Lists the files on a dump volume
echo	Echoes arguments
ed	Line-oriented text editor
enable	Enables spooling on a printer
env	Sets environment for command execution
eqn	Mathematical equation formatter
explain	Suggests alternatives to awkward phrases in text
expr	Evaluates expressions
factor	Factors a number
false	Returns a false value
file	Determines file type
find	Searches for files
finger	Lists personal information about users
get	Gets a version of an SCCS file
getopt	Parses command options
grep	Selects lines of a file based on pattern matching
haltsys	Immediately shuts down the system
hd	Prints a hexadecimal dump of a file
head	Outputs the first part of a file
help	Asks for help
hyphen	Finds hyphenated words
id	Outputs user and group id's and names
join	Joins two tabular data files
kill	Terminates or signals processes
lc	Lists directory contents in columns
ld	Link editor
lex	Generates lexical analysis routines
line	Copies a line from standard input to output
lint	C language syntax checker
ln	Links file names
login	Admits authorized users to a system
logname	Outputs the user's login name
look	Finds lines in a sorted file

lorder	Finds the ordering relation for an object library
lpr	Line printer spooler
ls	Lists contents of directories
m4	Macro processor
mail	Sends and receives /XENIX mail
make	Regenerates groups of programs
makekey	Generates an encryption key
man	Prints on-line manual entries
mesg	Permits or denies messages
mkdir	Makes a directory
mkfs	Builds a XENIX file system
mknod	Builds a XENIX special file (e.g., a printer or terminal)
mkstr	Creates an error message file
mkuser	Adds a new user to the system
mm	Text-formatting macros
mmt	Typesetting macros
more	Displays a file a screen at a time
mount	Attaches a file system to the root file system
mv	Moves files
netutil	Administers the mail network
newgrp	Changes active group membership
news	Prints news items
nice	Runs a program at reduced priority
nl	Line-numbering filter
nm	Prints names from a common object file
nohup	Runs a program immune from hang-ups and quits
nroff	Text formatter
od	Outputs an octal dump of a file
pack	Packs files
passwd	Changes a user's password
paste	Merges lines of files
pcat	Concatenates packed files
pcc	Portable C compiler
pr	Prints files
prof	Outputs execution profile data
prs	Prints an SCCS file
ps	Outputs process status

pstat	Prints information about processes, devices, etc.
ptx	Generates a permuted index
pwadmin	Performs password aging administration
pwck	Checks the integrity of the /etc/passwd file
pwd	Prints the name of the current working directory
quot	Summarizes file system ownership
random	Random number generator
ratfor	Compiler for a dialect of FORTRAN
rcp	Remote file copy program
regcmp	Regular expression compiler
remote	Executes a command on a remote system
rm	Removes file names
rmdir	Removes directories
rmdel	Removes an SCCS delta
rmuser	Removes a user from the system
rsh	Restricted XENIX system shell
sact	Prints current SCCS editing activity
sccsdiff	Compares two versions of an SCCS file
sddate	Sets the dump date
sdiff	Compares two files
sed	Stream editor
setmnt	Establishes the table of mounted file systems
settime	Changes file access and modification times
sh	The Bourne shell
shutdown	Performs an orderly system shutdown
size	Prints the sizes of object files
sleep	Suspends execution for a time interval
sort	Sorts and merges files
spell	Finds spelling errors
spline	Interpolates smooth curves
split	Splits a file
strings	Finds printable strings in a binary file
strip	Removes symbol table information from an object file
stty	Sets terminal characteristics
style	Analyzes readability of text
su	Temporarily changes user-id
sum	Outputs checksum and block count for a file
sync	Writes disk buffers to disk

sysadmin	Controls backup/restore operation
tail	Outputs the last part of a file
tar	Tape file archiving
tbl	Table formatter
tee	Pipe fitter
test	Evaluates conditions
time	Times command execution
timex	Times command execution
touch	Updates access and modification times of a file
tr	Character translation filter
troff	Phototypesetter text formatter
true	Returns a true value
tset	Sets terminal type
tsort	Topological sort
tty	Outputs the name of a terminal
umask	Sets file creation mode mask
umount	Detaches a previously mounted file system
uname	Outputs the name of the current XENIX system
unget	Ungets an SCCS file
uniq	Outputs a file with unique lines
units	Performs units conversions
unpack	Unpacks packed files
uuclean	Cleans up the uucp spool directory
uucp	Copies files between UNIX/XENIX systems
uulog	Outputs uucp log information
uuname	outputs uucp names of known systems
uustat	Outputs uucp status information
uuto	Copies files between UNIX/XENIX systems
uupick	Selects uucp files for processing
uux	Executes a command on a remote UNIX/XENIX system
val	Validates SCCS files
vi	Full-screen text editor
vsh	Visual shell
wait	Waits for completion of background processes
wall	Sends a message to all users
wc	Outputs line, word, and character counts for a file
what	Searches SCCS files for embedded comments
who	Outputs information on current users

whodo	Displays information about what each user is doing on the system
write	Sends messages to another user
xargs	Constructs an argument list and executes a command
xstr	Extracts strings from a C program
yacc	A compiler-generating tool
yes	Writes *yes* to the output file

Appendix C

XENIX System Files

/etc/passwd	User name and password file
/etc/group	User group file
/etc/rc	System start-up script
/etc/ttys	Login terminals table
/etc/motd	Message-of-the-day file
/etc/profile	Bourne shell login script
/etc/termcap	Terminal capability data base
/etc/ttytype	Serial line terminal types table
/etc/checklist	**fsck** file system list
/etc/mnttab	Mounted file system table
/usr/lib/crontab	Automatic program execution table
/etc/default/*	Default program information files
/etc/systemid	Micnet system name file
/usr/lib/mail/top	Micnet topology table
/usr/lib/mail/aliases	Micnet aliases table

Index

237

More Computer Knowledge from Que

LOTUS SOFTWARE TITLES
- 1-2-3 for Business $16.95
- 1-2-3 Macro Library 19.95
- 1-2-3 Tips, Tricks, and Traps 16.95
- Using 1-2-3 .... 17.95
- Using 1-2-3 Workbook and Disk 29.95
- Using Symphony 19.95

WORD-PROCESSING TITLES
- Improve Your Writing with Word Processing 12.95
- Using DisplayWrite 16.95
- Using MultiMate 16.95
- Using WordPerfect 16.95

IBM TITLES
- IBM PC Expansion & Software Guide, 5th Edition 21.95
- IBM PCjr Favorite Programs Explained 12.95
- IBM's Personal Computer, 2nd Edition 17.95
- Introducing IBM PCjr 12.95
- Networking IBM PCs: A Practical Guide 18.95
- PC DOS User's Guide 16.95
- PC DOS Workbook and Disk 29.95
- PC DOS Workbook Instructor's Guide 12.94
- Real Managers Use Personal Computers! 14.95

APPLICATIONS SOFTWARE TITLES
- Multiplan Models for Business 15.95
- Spreadsheet Software: From VisiCalc to 1-2-3 .... 15.95
- SuperCalc SuperModels for Business 16.95
- VisiCalc Models for Business 16.95

COMPUTER SYSTEMS TITLES
- Apple Favorite Programs Explained 12.95
- Introducing the Apple IIc 12.95
- Commodore 64 Favorite Programs Explained 12.95
- DEC Personal Computers Expansion & Software Guide 19.95
- The HP Touchscreen 19.95
- MS-DOS User's Guide 16.95
- TI-99/4A Favorite Programs Explained 12.95
- The First Book of ADAM (Coleco) 12.95
- The Second Book of ADAM: Using SmartWRITER 10.95

PROGRAMMING AND TECHNICAL TITLES
- C Programmer's Library 19.95
- C Programming Guide 19.95
- CP/M Programmer's Encyclopedia 19.95
- CP/M Software Finder 14.95
- Understanding XENIX: A Conceptual Guide 19.95

Que Order Line: 1-800-428-5331

All prices subject to change without notice.

LEARN MORE ABOUT C AND UNIX